Manage Me,
Manage You

Manage Me, Manage You

Managing people how they
want to be managed

ZAHOOR BARGIR

authorHOUSE®

AuthorHouse™ UK Ltd.
1663 Liberty Drive
Bloomington, IN 47403 USA
www.authorhouse.co.uk
Phone: 0800.197.4150

Published by AuthorHouse 02/19/2014

ISBN: 978-1-4817-9333-9 (sc)
ISBN: 978-1-4817-9334-6 (e)

Library of Congress Control Number: 2013923483

Any people depicted in stock imagery provided by Thinkstock are
models, and such images are being used for illustrative purposes only.
Certain stock imagery © Thinkstock.

This book is printed on acid-free paper.

Contents

Preface

Treat people as you want to be treated

This is a saying that has been around for as long as any one of us can remember. We've all heard somebody (probably your mother) say it as we grew up. But I took issue with this saying many moons ago. I realised that how I want to be treated is not necessarily how others want to be treated and vice versa. And this is the thinking behind this book: to treat others in the way *they* want to be treated.

Whether at work or at home, we all want to be seen and be appreciated for the individuals we are. Out of all the managers that I have worked with over the years the ones that have treated me as a valued individual have been my favourites. Yes, there is the notion of fairness, of treating no one team member more favourably than another, but that is different to treating everyone uniformly. By treating everyone the same way and using one management technique to manage all, you detract from people's unique qualities. Some people want your attention and some people want to be left alone to get on with the job. How can you tell who wants what?

This book is for managers in business who want to develop their own management styles. Successful managers are not borne of just one style. Different situations require different styles, and we all have our own preferred way of working and managing. Often, our preferred way of managing is effective with some people, and not with others.

- So how can I tell what works and what doesn't?
- Is there a formula I can use to understand someone else's style?
- Can I use this to develop and discover untapped potential?

Through the DISC profiling system, we can get to know our preferred working style and understand what works for others.

Management is a word that conjures up different meanings depending on who you're speaking to. Some people make management in the workplace look easy and others don't really have a clue. If you ask successful managers about their style of management you will find each person has their own style. Management schools and theorists highlight various styles and suggest different types of management depending on different scenarios. But what many of them don't mention is the individual. What about you as a person and manager? Should your management style be something that comes naturally to you or can you develop a mixture of styles?

For nearly two decades, I have worked with countless managers who have had varying degrees of success in their chosen fields. Whether working in finance, marketing, sales, operations or I.T., there isn't one style of management that can be said to have a monopoly of success over another.

The foundation of this book is the DISC profiling model that has been around for decades and peppered throughout are real-life illustrations of management scenarios. These have been gathered from my own experiences and those of other managers.

The essence of this book is to focus on you. You have your own strengths, weaknesses, motivations etc. When you look slightly deeper, you'll recognise that they form certain patterns that are unique to you.

Whatever your own style of management, one thing is for certain: the people you manage will most likely be different to you. They will have their own strengths, weaknesses and motivations. Understanding and tapping into each of these different areas will bring out the best in them and enable you to achieve your goals.

Through understanding the DISC profiling system and how it works, you will realise that you don't need to understand people's deep psychological make-up to be able to bring out the best in them. And if this book helps you bring out the best in yourself and others around you, then it has met its objective.

Ultimately, getting to where we want to be requires everyone to be pulling or pushing in the same direction. Throughout history, great success stories (whether individual or as a group) have all come about through teamwork. And teamwork, ultimately, begins with you.

Acknowledgements

It was quite a journey getting this book to completion and it wouldn't have been done without the constant love and support of my parents, my beautiful siblings and friends—you are my world. I have learnt so much with and from you and continue to do so. I also have a host of people to thank who have, directly or indirectly, made an impact on my producing this book.

Firstly, to my teachers: Ian McDonald, Patrick Lynch, Jackson White and Sh. Haytham Tamim. You inspired me to see and appreciate my talents and have the confidence to develop and follow my own ideas.

I also wish to thank the following people for their excellent work and support. A big thank you to my editor, Kate Turvey for her great suggestions and professional guidance. To my book designer, Aneesa Dalwai who was so easy to work with as always and knows how to convert ideas into an image. To Rebecca Carter who was patient with me, especially when I dragged my feet in finishing the book. To London House for their support, especially during those late nights in the library. To Dr Nasima Hassan for her academic guidance and to Nadia Butt for the photography. To Bev James who really helped me see the power of DISC profiling in her fun way. And finally to Aiman Al-Maimani and Jonathan Jay who inspired me to kick-start my writing.

I also thank the people who have enabled me to put all I have learnt into practice. To all the managers I've had the pleasure of working with throughout my professional career and those I have interviewed, thank you for sharing your experiences. I have learnt much from you and will no doubt continue to do so. To my life teachers who have shared their wisdom and teachings: William Moulton Marston, Dr Stephen R Covey, Tony Robbins, Dr Tony Alessandra, David W Merrill and William H Bates (physician). You have been truly inspirational as leaders and I am grateful for all I have learnt from you.

Chapter 1

Managing yourself

'First Seek to Understand, then to be Understood'
Stephen Covey

There's a saying that employees don't leave companies, they leave managers. If this is the case, then it's no surprise as an employee's relationship with their direct line manager is the single most important factor in employee engagement. With business failures at record rates, motivating your team and retaining your best staff has never been as crucial to business success as it is now. Staff turnover is expensive and despite what some managers may think, most employees don't move primarily for more money. A poll[1] showed that of those that chose to resign voluntarily around 75% would move on for issues related with their management and only roughly 22% would move for reasons of pay.

Companies typically invest heavily in training their top level management to bring out the best in their people, but less so for aspiring managers or middle management. This means that most new managers struggle to manage diverse teams as they tend to employ the one management style they know—usually the style they themselves liked to be managed. However, we need more versatile managers in business. Why? Because:

- One style of management will not work for everyone in your team
- People have different motivations
- People like to work in different ways
- People have different strengths and weaknesses

There are so many variables to managing people, is it any wonder we can get it so wrong?

---

[1] Poll conducted by Gallup http://businessjournal.gallup.com/content/106912/turning-around-your-turnover-problem.aspx#1

Having great technical skills may have gotten you promoted, but it isn't necessarily going to keep your team motivated or help you in retaining your best staff. With the job market being the most fluid it has ever been, staff are expecting to be managed in a way that suits their needs, and managers have to be versatile enough to meet these expectations.

Here I will show you the ways to identify what management style works with some people and what works with others.

This book has two main aims:

1. To understand yourself better: your strengths, weaknesses and preferences.
2. To recognise and understand the dimensions of other people's styles, so that you can adapt your own style to get the results you want.

Underlying all this is a tool called DISC. With the DISC tool, you will get to understand how you can tackle all of the above and more. It will give you an understanding of yourself and your preferred behavioural style and how your style impacts upon others around you. You will also establish an understanding of others' styles and how this affects you. This book is for people who want to communicate better with everyone they interact with at all levels. It is about concentrating more on the process to achieve the desired outcome.

All of us want to be heard by the other person, whether at home or at work, and we will be using the principles of DISC to explore better ways of getting what we want from others in the workplace.

So let's get right into it.

A Brief Introduction to DISC

Let us begin with what the acronym DISC stands for:

D - Dominance
I - Influence
S - Steady
C - Conscientious

The DISC behavioural system is based on the work of the pioneering psychologist, Dr William M Marston. In his book, *Emotions of Normal People*[2], he described how behaviour can be categorised into segments and how each of these segments describes a certain way of behaving which we adopt to get by in life. The concept of categorising into segments isn't a new one but has evolved over many centuries in a variety of different ways. Effectively, whether it is Fire, Water, Air and Earth or Introverted and Extroverted, each of the evolutions of behavioural theory have centred around certain characterised segments from Hippocrates, 'the father of medicine', in 460 BC through to Carl Gustav Jung and Dr William M Marston in the early twentieth century. Today, even with advances in science and medicine, the basic ideas of Hippocrates are still referred to by many.

In this book we'll be concentrating on DISC from a work and management perspective. As highlighted above, DISC is made up of four main segments—Dominance, Influence, Steady and Conscientious—and you can think of these four segments as parts of a wheel. All the segments constitute the making of the wheel and signify the four types we are going to discuss in the coming chapters. Figure 1.1 represents the four different styles, however, it is important to note that people have varying levels of each style in their behaviour, unlike the diagram where each style section is shown as equal.

Over the years, many iterations of DISC and what the acronym stands for have been developed. For the purpose of this book, we'll keep the four segments as follows:

Dominance = D-style
Influence = I-style
Steady = S-style
Conscientious = C-style

---

[2] Marston, W.M. (1928), *Emotions of Normal People* (Devonshire Press)

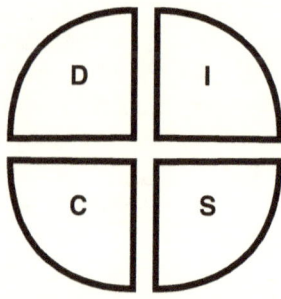

Fig. 1.1 DISC is formed of four main sections

There are four main sections to this wheel. The main axes consist of Direct, Indirect, Task and People and are highlighted in Fig. 1.2.

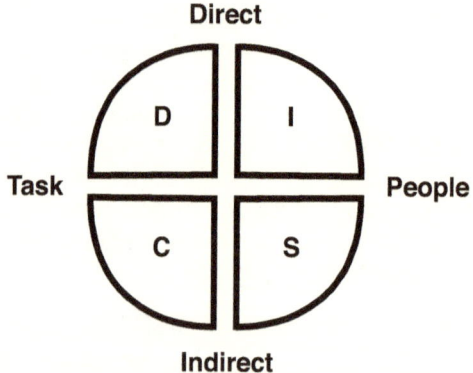

Fig. 1.2 Diagram showing the four main axes of DISC

This wheel can be split two ways, horizontally and vertically. If we split it into two segments (see Fig. 1.3), the upper segment (D-style and I-style) shows the styles that are direct in their ways and the lower segment (S-style and C-style) highlight the styles that are more indirect in behaviour.

Direct

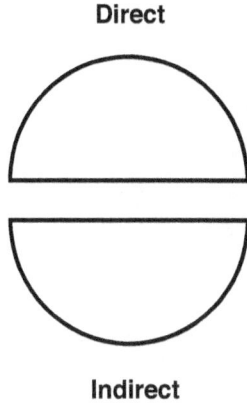

Indirect

Fig. 1.3

In Figure 1.3, these two elements (Direct, Indirect) consider how the various styles interact with their environment and what influence they believe they have over their environment.

Direct/Indirect

Direct—Dominance and Influence

The direct half indicates that these styles like to take control over their immediate environment. They believe that they need to be 'actively engaged' with their surroundings for something to happen. So they'll go out and make themselves known to all around them. More extroverted by nature, staying in the background is not something the direct person chooses to do.

Confidence isn't something the direct style lacks. They are self-assured of their skills and if they want something they will go out and get it. They tend to believe they have more influence than their more 'indirect' counterparts and aren't afraid to be 'seen' to be doing things.

Indirect—Steady and Conscientious

As the name suggests, the indirect half prefers to operate this way, indirectly. The indirect half is more distinct by its understatedness. Not ones to rush, they like to take their time and do things in a more passive manner. They are more reserved than their direct counterparts and prefer to use caution as opposed to jumping in head-first. They like to think things through before making their move or settling on a decision.

Some might describe the indirect styles as less confident, although they may outwardly display less emotion and confidence, this doesn't mean they feel any less emotional and confident inside. This is a less assertive style and they would rather have their actions speak louder than their words.

Reserved by nature, they prefer to operate behind the scenes than on the frontline in contrast to their direct counterparts who thrive as the figureheads of their domain.

Task/People

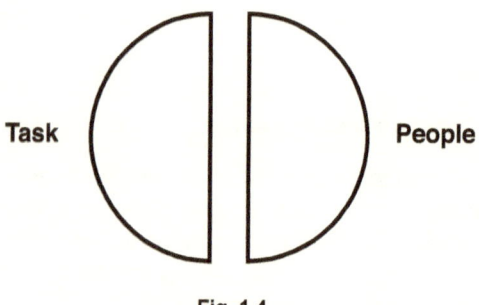

Fig. 1.4

In Figure 1.4, these two elements (Task, People) illustrate what someone's main focus is.

Task—Dominance and Conscientious

The Task section of the diagram highlights the styles that are more task oriented. They usually have their full focus on the task at hand and everything they do is from this point of view. People with a task focus are easy to spot. Listen to the words that they use—there will be more 'doing' and 'factual' words in their conversation. Here are some examples:

'I need to make 50 calls today no matter what.'
'It just doesn't add up, the numbers don't support the argument.'
'The model needs to show that it is working.'
'There is a flaw in the system and this needs to be solved by the close of today.'
'Regardless of sleep, I get up as the job needs to be done.'

The focus of each of these comments is on the task at hand, and what's missing is any mention of feelings. Process, targets or results take priority for the task-focused person. This person is unlikely to stop at 'I gave it my best shot'. For them, they need to get a result and if their best isn't good enough then they will find another way of getting the result that they want.

Being task-focused could also mean that they are more adept at dealing with systems rather than human beings. In fact, the two task-focused styles (D-style, C-style—more on these later) may view the human element of a system to be the weak link, as people are more prone to making 'silly' errors than systems. The task-focused style would rather have no human interference in the system at all.

People—Influence and Steady

The People side of the axis shows the two styles that are more people-oriented. The human element in any process is very important to these types. So for them, they may find it more difficult to make people redundant in an organisation, regardless of whether it's absolutely crucial for the survival of the business. Rather than merely the cost factor, they also see the people factor involved.

The people section also describes how people-focused styles' behaviours are influenced by certain factors. The people-focused styles (I-style, S-style) feel comfortable dealing with people. For them, they like to connect with others in the workplace. They prefer to go with their feelings and this can also be evident in the words they use. Here are some examples:

'I feel it just doesn't quite hit the spot.'
'Let's all get together and give it a go!'

'Let's do this, it'll look so good.'
'Personally, if it means the team benefits, then I don't mind doing this.'

People-focused styles are less inclined to want to spend all day in front of a spreadsheet. This might be more of a task-focused style's ideal day at work but those with people styles will want to have conversations and engage with others as it makes their work more enjoyable.

Based upon these findings, the DISC system has evolved and there are several companies who have refined Dr Marston's ideas to develop their own version based on their own research and findings. Whatever the subtle differences between each of these versions of DISC, they all have a common denominator in that they are measuring, in some way, the observable behaviour of the person rather than a person's internal psychological make-up which requires a rather deeper assessment.

Herein lies the beauty of the system. The DISC system can be used to ascertain someone's behavioural preference by listening to what they say or by observing their physical actions. There is little need to figure out why a person acts this way or said such a thing. This takes time and requires plenty of study and knowledge. The DISC system incorporates a process that looks purely at behaviour that is outwardly expressed and observable.

Just like any tool, however, it is best used as an indicative measure, albeit a highly accurate one. This way snap judgements are kept at bay and leaves open the avenue of learning more about the other person the more time you spend with them.

In short, this is how each character style is broken down:

D-style - Direct and Task
I-style - Direct and People
S-style - Indirect and People
C-style - Indirect and Task

Attract or Repel?

Have you ever experienced differences with someone based on how they act? If you haven't, then you are probably the only one living never to have done so. At times, behaviour that we don't recognise and aren't familiar with can throw us off track. Consider this...

You are in the company of someone you met just ten minutes ago and already you find yourself wondering how to get away from them. On the other hand, you may have just met someone ten minutes previously and you're getting on like you've known each other for years. Before you know it, hours have gone by and it still feels like hardly any time has passed, so easy has been the conversation.

Whether it's instant rapport or a clash of styles, one thing stands out—one situation attracts you to whereas the other repels you from the person. Ultimately, who you get on with and who you don't is a subjective thing. Sometimes it is 'birds of a feather flock together' and sometimes it is 'opposites attract'. And this is relevant for situations at work and at home.

There is another way

Knowing that we won't necessarily have instant rapport with everyone is a step towards appreciating others for their differences. Through appreciation of other ways of being, we open up to opportunities to see another viewpoint—someone else may spot something that you don't. We can then begin to appreciate our own strengths and weaknesses and focus on the things we can do something about (ourselves), rather than worry about the things we can't (other people).

The saying 'every positive action has an opposite reaction' shows us that regardless of our strengths there is also a downside to what we are doing. For example, not having much patience in traffic jams, a senior manager I know decided to study the roads of London (satnav systems don't necessarily work that well in central London) and seek out other routes of getting from A to B.

Over time, he got to know many shortcuts and alternative routes. It saved him enormous amounts of time as he bypassed much of the traffic. However, a by-product of his increased knowledge of the back streets of London, which can be full of potholes and uneven surfaces, has been more nails and other sharp objects getting stuck into his tyres. This past year, he mentioned he has taken his car to the garage quite a few times to either fix a puncture or replace his tyres altogether.

Acknowledging this has made me acutely aware that each of our behavioural styles have positive and not-so-positive elements to them. Differences between us may, therefore, have more of a complementary element than we can appreciate.

With the DISC tool, we are able to see what these differences with others are and what we can do to capitalise on them.

Things to consider are:

- How you can start to become more self-aware.
- Where you are coming from and how this measures up to someone else and how they behave.
- What you can do to make the other person feel more comfortable with you, even though your styles may be at opposite ends of the scale.

This system has helped millions around the world come to terms with their own style and those of others, with the result of creating better personal and working relationships. You too can benefit from the system, so…

Which style are you?

> *'He who knows others is learned.*
> *He who knows himself is wise.'*
> Lao Tse

This chapter is all about understanding your own natural style, the one you are most comfortable with. Being social creatures, we interact with people of all styles which inevitably rubs off on us as individuals. It is, therefore, very rare to find someone who is exclusively one style and no other. Every one of us has elements of all the styles. So we all cover the D, I, S and C styles in some way and in different situations. However, being unique individuals, we have all developed our own preferred style over the years that has come about through both nature and nurture. How much is nature and how much is nurture can be left for another day. What is important to acknowledge, however, is that we all have our own preferred style and that no style is better or worse than another.

In this section, you are going to participate in a quick assessment. There are no right or wrong answers and it's important to see this as only an indication of what your style may be. For the actual DISC assessment, constructed over years of careful research and which will give you a more detailed and accurate assessment of your style, log onto the website www.companybasix.com and see for yourself. Think of yourself as the launch pad from where everything begins.

On the next page is a table with 12 statements. Against each statement are 4 different options - a, b, c and d. Consider each option and give it a number from 4 to 1. (not duplicating any number i.e. once you have put a number 3 next to an option, this has been used and you can then only place 1, 2 and 4 against the other remaining three options)

4 = Most like you
3 = Like you
2 = Not really like you
1 = Least like you

Be sure to put a number against each of the four options, not leaving any blanks. To help you decide, follow these simple steps.

Step 1
Put yourself in a neutral state of mind. Take a deep breath, and clear your mind.

Step 2

Focus on a work situation only. This is important because the 'hat' we have on at home could be, or most likely will be, different from the 'hat' we have on at work. And for the purposes of consistency and accuracy, it is good to have that one situation in mind when going through the four various options.

Remember:

Do not spend too much time on each question. Go with your instinct and move on.

Go through the four options in each of the 12 statements and fill them in with numbers 1-4, in order of your preference (without duplicating any numbers). The top line has been filled in as an example.

When all the boxes have been filled in with a number, total each column at the bottom and then plot the totals on the diagram over the page.

At work, I like to operate at a ___ pace	Fast and competitive	2	Fast and exciting	1	Steady and relaxed	3	Slow and methodical	4
Now fill in the rest of the table below when you are ready								
1) My desk is usually...	a) Piled with papers with many projects on the go		b) Cluttered and a bit messy, but I know where things are		c) Ambient and personal		d) Tidy and orderly	
2) I like to work at a ___ pace	a) Fast and Competitive		b) Fast and exciting		c) Steady and relaxed		d) Deliberate and methodical	
3) When I'm working on something, I prefer to...	a) Just do it, or delegate it to someone else		b) See if someone can do it better than me, and ask them politely to help me out		c) Watch someone do it, or show me how to do it and I can take it from there		d) Work out why we are doing it, and then figure out for myself a better way of doing it	
4) At work, I would describe myself as	a) Competitive and focused		b) Inspired and energised		c) Relaxed and friendly		d) Meticulous and logical	
5) When I speak at work, I am usually...	a) Direct and straight to the point		b) High in energy and dynamic		c) Friendly and steady		d) Calm, thoughtful and considered	
6) When I communicate with colleagues, my body language tends to be...	a) Efficient, assertive and maybe at times combative		b) Open, expressive and tactile. Much hand and body movement		c) Friendly and personal		d) Conservative and neutral. Non-contact orientated	
7) When it comes to decision-making, I tend to be...	a) Quick and decisive		b) Instant and impulsive		c) Slow and indecisive		d) Needing all facts to make a decision	
8) In a group, I tend to see myself as...	a) The leader and driven to find solutions		b) An ideas person and quite creative		c) A team-player and willing to help out wherever possible		d) Making sure discussions are relevant and ideas thought through properly with balanced consideration	
9) Under pressure, I initially tend to...	a) Give out more orders to ensure everyone is doing what they are supposed to		b) Lose my patience easier with those around me		c) Go quiet and get on with the work		d) Withdraw and prefer my own space	
10) When I go on a training course where I don't know anyone, I tend to...	a) Know I'm there for a purpose, so I get what I'm there for and get out		b) Enjoy meeting new people and I am totally comfortable introducing myself		c) Take a seat and I am friendly when others approach me		d) Be prepared and take lots of notes	
11) I am generally motivated by...	a) Targets and achievement		b) Recognition and popularity		c) Safety and security		d) Getting things right	
12) When I come to actual work...	a) I don't like routine activities		b) I am good at starting projects, although they often remain incomplete		c) Routine tasks don't bother me		d) I complete what I've started	
Add your totals for columns here	D =		I =		S =		C =	

Table 1 Fill in this table to discover your style

13

Once you have totalled up each of the four columns, plot your scores on the diagram below.

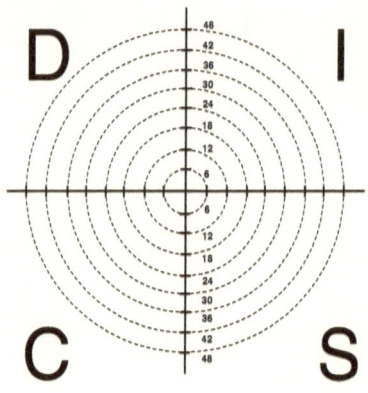

For example:

D = 40
I = 28
S = 10
C = 6

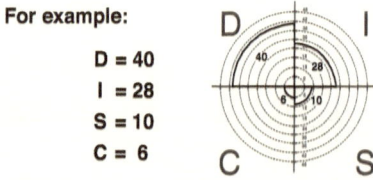

Plot your scores here. What do they show?

The highest number is your Primary dominant style. Anything over 24 can be considered a high (or above average) score. The second highest number is your Secondary dominant style. So what do your results mean?

From the graph you are able to see your main dominant styles. The example above shows someone with a high D/I.

To understand someone else and where they are along the DISC spectrum, we need to have a benchmark as we individuals all approach life from a unique perspective. For instance, a colleague may perceive a workmate as being obsessed with detail, but you may find that this same person is not really that detail focused at all. We all come from our unique perspectives and how we judge a person depends very much on where we stand ourselves. Once we have been able to look at and analyse ourselves, we also get a better understanding of where others are in comparison to us.

For example: if I was driving along the highway in my car at a steady 60 mph and a car passed me travelling at 70 mph, it would seem like they were creeping past me. However, if I stood still and this car was travelling at 70 mph, it would zoom by very quickly. In both cases the other car was travelling at 70 mph but in the second instance we perceive it to be going much faster because of the comparison with our own starting position. To know and understand our own position helps us to put someone else's into context.

Summary

Are you Direct or Indirect?

Direct

Like to be engaged with their surroundings
They like something, so they go for it
Self-assured.

Indirect

They tend to be more passive
More cautious by nature
Prefer to think things through before acting

Are you Task or People?

Task

Focus is on getting things done
More systems-oriented in their thinking
Focus tends to be on achievement.

People

Other people's feelings matter to them
They get things done through people
Focus tends to be on building relationships.

Chapter 2

What are the DISC principles?

We will be looking at the four main style-types throughout this book and we will focus on what this means for you. In our everyday lives, each of us comes across people who display some feature of each of the different behavioural types. The office is no different.

It's a typical Monday in the office and Dave has just walked in. It is 10.30 a.m. and he walks in with purpose, ready for the day. The others, Ian, Sue and Christine are already in the office and have been working away since 9 a.m. Every Monday at 11 a.m. there is a weekly team catch-up so they all know that, in addition to going over what happened in the past week, they will also be reviewing targets for the coming week. Being a Finance office, they often have to meet daily deadlines and it's important for them to know where the team is in terms of progress. It is the busiest time of the month for the department as they are just assessing the month-end financial position and late nights are currently common.

Apart from his initial office greeting, Dave doesn't have much more to say. He's focused on getting on with his day as he has plenty of meetings to attend and he's always got 101 things going on—it's hard to keep up with him at the best of times. His desk has piles of paper everywhere and a big stack of business cards that he seems to collect for fun. Then there is Ian, who is constantly on the phone and this has become a prickly subject between Dave and Ian. Ian, however, insists being on the phone enables him to fulfil his role. It's no surprise that he tends to spend long hours in the office, probably trying to catch up with his day job after spending so much of it socialising during work hours. It's almost as if he's got used to this way of working, as it certainly hasn't curtailed his socialising in the office.

In the corner with her head down is Sue. Gently spoken, she's ever-present at her desk and you'd be lucky to get a squeak out of her. She's easily the most reliable and any of the jobs the others don't want to do, Sue is certain to take on. As long as she knows what to do, she'll just do it—one could say a saviour of the office. Finally, you have Christine. She is affectionately known as the 'Guru' as technically she's brilliant and knows all the details of the financials. People from all the other offices constantly call her with work-related questions and she's another person who seems to spend all day in the office. It seems the spreadsheet is an extension of her arm. She's mastered its functionality and it often takes ages to open a spreadsheet as she's always overloading each document with formulas. Change one thing on the spreadsheet and Christine will certainly get to know about it. Dave loves her for it as he can always rely on her.

Wherever we are and whoever we work with, we can all recognise a certain style in our colleagues. Although the DISC behavioural system shows four main categories, the majority of us have two main dominant styles.

What is the D-style?

'You're Fired!'
Donald Trump (*The Apprentice*)

What is this type like?

The D-style can often be described as:

Driven
Aggressive
Goal-oriented
Focused
Decisive
Task-focused
Quick

Famous D-styles include:

Bernie Ecclestone—Formula 1 racing founder and owner
Simon Cowell—Founder of TV show *X-Factor* and other talent shows
Arnold Schwarzenegger—Actor/governor/body builder
Alan Sugar—Billionaire businessman/TV personality

Traits of the D-style personality

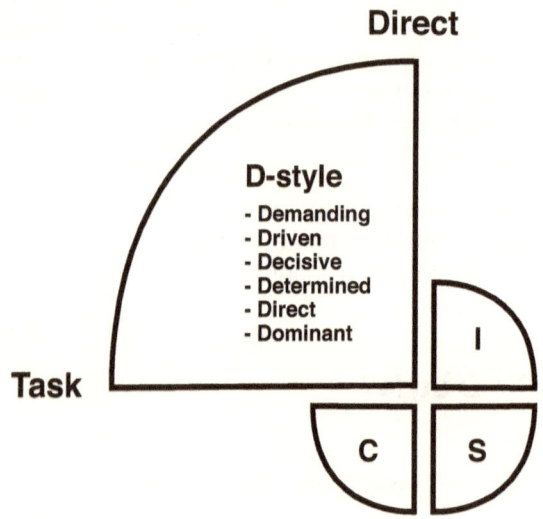

Fig. 2.1 Traits of the D-style

In the DISC quadrant, the D-style forms the part of the top left which constitutes Direct and Task (see Fig. 2.1).

With their ability to take in the facts quickly, make decisions based on these and to be more outcome-focused, the D-style personality is predominantly a left-brained operator. If something doesn't make sense they will be quick to mention it and in no uncertain terms either.

When they communicate, they don't beat around the bush and they like to say it how they see it. To many others the D-style may, with their straightforward approach, come across as abrupt. This is largely due to their focus on the task at hand coupled with wanting to find quick answers to their questions.

Direct behaviour

The D-style wants control of their surroundings. If they do not have control, then they make it so that they have. In an interview with the *Sunday Times* newspaper, Bernie Ecclestone (a classic D-style personality) said 'I feel I have to be in control... I've tied up a lot of things in the sport... by controlling the way things are run, by everyone knowing what they should be doing.'

As this style's name suggests, the D-style personality is one that likes to lead. D-styles aren't satisfied with the status quo and, rightly or wrongly, if they see something they don't like they will go and do something about it.

They aren't averse to bending the rules, especially if the rules prevent them from reaching their target. And because they see themselves as powerful and able to get things done, in terms of their environment and surroundings, they usually always want things to go their own way. If things don't go as they would have liked, then they'll do everything in their power to ensure they do.

Task-focused

Being task-oriented, the D-style person sets targets for themselves and takes action to achieve them. Power and control are both important to the D-style personality as they play an important role in getting things done.

When it comes to decision-making, the D-style will often look at the main facts and make their decision based on these. D-styles don't need to be bombarded with much detail. As long as they have the essentials which show the pros and cons of an idea, they will have enough to say yay or nay.

In their pursuit of a goal, the D-style will make this goal their main focus. So much so, that everything else just becomes incidental to them achieving this goal. There isn't usually much regard for anyone else's feelings because 'when things have to get done, they get done'. Relationships can, therefore, become strained as a result. They like to have many balls up in the air at the same time. When you are speaking with them, they are likely to take another call just in case there is something else they need to spend their time on. Such is their capacity to take on many different things, they can start something and move onto something else, leaving others to complete the work they started.

They can be fiercely competitive and the D-style person likes their surroundings to shout out success and achievement. So trophies and pictures with powerful people might adorn their offices.

The D-style has a kind of 'shield' around them when it comes to personal interactions. They can be focused on the task at hand and follow it through, even if the task or choice of action is going to be unpopular with those around them. They have a knack for not being too affected by personal attacks from others as it is the goal that is their main focus.

Weaknesses

- They skip over the small print and can get caught out later
- Over-confidence
- Taking on too much
- Timekeeping is not their strong point
- Not sensitive to others' feelings.

What is the I-style?

> '*All work and no play makes Jack a dull boy*'
> Anonymous

What is this type like?

The I-style can often be described as:

Socialiser
Interactor
Playful
Open

Exhibitionist
Tactile
Networker

Famous I-styles include:

Jim Carrey—Actor/stand-up comedian
Jonathan Ross—Talk show host/radio DJ
Eddie Murphy—Actor/stand-up comedian

Traits of the I-style personality

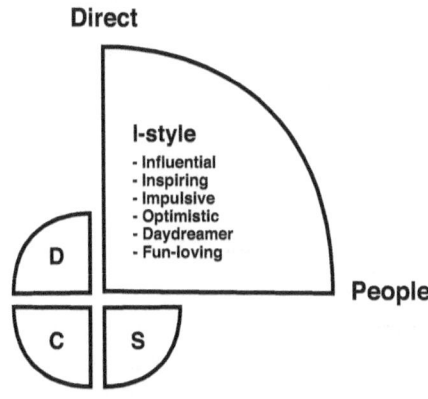

Fig. 2.2 Traits of the I-style

In the DISC quadrant, the I-style personality is top-right and includes the elements Direct and People (see Fig. 2.2).

With their emotional and creative strengths, the I-style person is good at connecting people. What people think about them is very important to the I-style. This is a type that gets their energy from people around them. They like to be the life and soul of the party and cannot sit back and blend into the background in a crowd. The I-style is the one who is likely to break the silence in a group. This person is the 'people-pleaser' and plays for approval from others. In fact, one of the biggest fears of the I-style is rejection. In his studies, William Marston and others since, have found that part of the make-up of the I-style is that they care very much what people think and say about them. In contrast, once a D-style has made a decision, they are capable of following through regardless of what others may think. The I-style, on the other hand, is likely to make a decision but, depending on what kind of reception they get from others, may even change their mind.

Direct behaviour

Just like the D-style, the I-style personality likes to have a direct impact on their immediate environment. Through their silky-smooth communication skills, the I-style will use their powers of persuasion to get their way and, more importantly, they believe they can do so.

With their natural enthusiasm, they are adept at influencing those around them and bringing others along on their journey. Pro-active and go-getters, they like to make openings for themselves to go out there and get new business. Just like an alchemist, the I-style is the one who will try to turn lead into gold. The I-style is the dreamer. They're likely to be the one who gets caught daydreaming at school but at other times will be busy entertaining the other kids.

Being the dreamer, the I-style will think up big things of what they can become. They'll convince everyone that this dream is achievable and they are so good at selling themselves there is no way you cannot believe them. They'll have some idea of how to get there, although they won't care too much about the details because one way or another, they know they can.

The world, to the I-style, really is their oyster and how far they go is up to them.

People-focused

The I-style likes being around people and telling stories, jokes etc. Because of their penchant for entertaining, they tend to naturally gravitate towards roles that put them at the heart of working with others in some way. Sales or customer-facing roles are usually the ones they go for. Something like accountancy, where you spend countless hours building complex spreadsheets, would probably feel a little solitary for the I-style. However, I do know I-styles who have made accountancy work for them and have thrived as finance managers. They have built a strong team around them with people who prefer to do the detailed work more than they do.

Being people-focused, the I-style prefers the 'soft' side of work to the technical aspect. The I-style tends to thrive when working in teams. They come into their own in this environment and are good at keeping the energy of the group up.

With their easy-going, fun style they are also good at encouraging their team. The D-style personalities may like to charge ahead regardless of how the team feels but the I-styles can assist in ensuring that the team is up for it and that individuals feel good whilst pursuing the vision. How others feel is important to the I-style as this all contributes to the overall morale of the team.

Tip: *Want to spot an I-style?*

How long does it take for them to say goodbye? If it's longer than the amount of time they were actually at the party, you have an I-style

---

Just like the D-style, the I-style person likes to have the freedom to express themselves. Neither likes being micro-managed and they both prefer to work with some leeway.

Weaknesses

- Lack of focus for sustained periods
- Can be careless with detail
- Care too much about what others think
- Wasteful with their energy socialising when it might be better spent working
- Timekeeping—goodbyes can take ages.

What is the S-style?

A bird in the hand is worth two in the bush
English Proverb

What is this type like?

The S-style can often be described as:

Loyal
Consistent
Team-player
Security-minded
Introverted
Self-conscious
Patient

Famous S-style personalities include:

Mahatma Gandhi—Lawyer and Indian activist leader
Princess Diana—British Royal
Michael Parkinson—Talk show host

Traits of the S-style personality

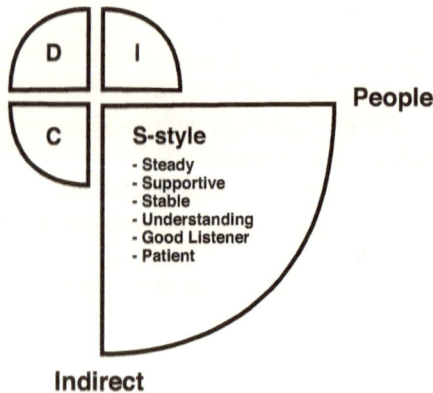

Fig. 2.3 Traits of the S-style

S-styles are usually the ones behind the scenes getting the job done. In Formula 1 or Nascar racing for example, the S-styles are the race team engineers: the ones who work day and night to get the cars ready for the drivers, but whose work goes largely unnoticed. Leadership isn't the preserve of just one style. Having said this, S-styles are comfortable following instructions and working as part of a team. So when it comes to decision-making, they don't mind taking the back seat and allowing others to take charge.

In terms of pace, they naturally tend to move slower or not with as much urgency in comparison to the D- or I-style. They tend to keep to themselves and focus mainly on the job at hand without interfering with what others are doing. That is the key here. They focus on doing the best job they can, for the role they have been assigned and don't want to let their team down. They are intent on keeping their side of the bargain in the way they are expected to.

The S-style tends to be more concerned about the process of doing something. They will say 'show me how to do it' and will then diligently continue doing it the way you have just shown them. Don't expect many histrionics from this type as what you see is generally what you get. They are unlikely to do something of their own volition for example just because they have found a much better way of doing something. If they find a better way, they might just keep it to themselves and disclose it only when they are certain it works better or if asked.

Indirect behaviour

As you can see from the diagram (see Fig. 2.3), the S-style occupies the bottom right-hand section of the grid which shows a combination of indirect and people-oriented attributes. The indirect behaviour indicator suggests when they interact with the external environment, they do so in a more passive way. The S-styles do not impose themselves on others around them. When they are at a party, they tend to wait for others to introduce themselves first. Contrast this with the I-styles who have a more direct approach and introduce themselves, even in a group, and revel in getting to know new people.

It isn't just at parties that the S-style person holds back, it can happen in dating too. I remember a friend of mine, an S-style, who met a girl at a friend's dinner party. He spoke to her very briefly but didn't take down her details; they just went their separate ways. Thankfully for him, he was part of a group email which also included the person he had met. He asked me how he could engage with her without emailing her directly. As an I-style, I would have contacted her directly, but he wasn't comfortable with that approach so I thought of a different way. I suggested that he might email the whole group and try to bring her into the conversation and see if she responded. Again, this made him uncomfortable because he didn't know everyone on the email list very well. In the end, we discussed getting in touch with a mutual friend who knew her, and they all went out for dinner together.

The S-style tends to be more comfortable staying out of the limelight. In fact, they often have a reactionary-style when it comes to interacting with their surroundings. They would rather be introduced by someone or have someone introduce themselves first, as well as preferring to take the backseat during meetings.

They like organisation; to be prepared before doing anything. One way to get on the wrong side of the S-style is to give them something to do and not show them how or brief them properly. The D-style trait of needing something to be done immediately with a vague outline of what needs doing because it is urgent doesn't go down well with the S-style. The slower-paced, more deliberate working style of the C-style personality (see below) is more to the S-style's liking. This way they have time to think things through and can then ready themselves for action.

When the S-style is ready for taking action they tend to see it through right to the very end. Not like the I-style, who can keep projects open and unfinished because they need to tend to something else, the S-style likes to complete one job before moving onto the next one.

The S-style person tends not to be demanding. They are more passive and trust others to make the right decision. Patience is something they usually have plenty of.

People-oriented

Just like the I-style, the people-side of things is one of the main drivers for the S-style. They can work on their own quite easily but prefer to see themselves belonging to a larger group. Returning to the earlier point about not wanting to impose themselves on others, the S-style will tend to put the group interests before their own. Their natural empathy for others means they often see things from the other person's perspective and takes their feelings into consideration first.

Due to their naturally inhibited style it may take them a while to build relationships in the workplace but when they do they tend to be more enduring. It can take a while for others to get to know them too. One of my team members was an S-style, let's call her Lisa. She had been with the company for about a year before I joined and over the course of the next few months I gradually got to hear what others thought of the individuals in my team. As part of Lisa's role, once a month she was expected to make a trip to head office and work with the central HQ team on some areas that needed attention for the month-end accounts. Lisa only communicated with those she had to. However, others in the extended team at HQ often misconstrued her quietness towards them as not 'getting on' with them. I could see this was not necessarily the case and it was more likely to do with her self-consciousness, so I mentioned that it was probably due to her style and shyness. They then began seeing her in another light. They saw the reason for her saying very little and accepted her as she was. In time, she also started speaking to them, one by one.

S-styles are good listeners and take an interest in others. This is how they connect which can make them valuable in times of change. The S-style person finds it easier to understand what others are going through who in turn find it easy to confide in them. Consequently, they often know more about what is happening on the 'shop-floor' than the managers do, but don't expect them to share this valuable information. Loyalty is also a trait the S-style values and if they have been told something in confidence, it tends to stay that way.

Their people skills help create a supportive environment that can enable team managers to take the step and work to their potential. In their own intimate way, they can instil confidence and give reassurance which can make a manager's role much easier when it comes to getting the best out of a team.

Tip: *DISC in a car*

D-style - The steering wheel and accelerator/brake
I-style - The style and feel of the car
S-style - The engine
C-style - The dials and the finish.

What is the C-style?

'It's only worth doing if it's done right'
Anonymous

What is this type like?

The C-style can often be described as:

Detail-oriented
Accurate
Logical
Critical thinker
Cautious
Compliant
Perfectionist

Famous C-style personalities include:

Tiger Woods—Professional golfer
Steve Jobs—CEO Apple Corp
Bill Gates—Microsoft founder
Jonny Wilkinson—England International rugby player

Traits of the C-style personality

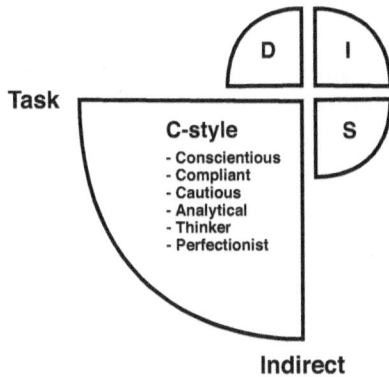

Fig. 2.4 Traits of the C-style

The C-style is the most detail-oriented of the four types. They tend to look for things to be correct and in their rightful positions. If the person you are speaking with tends to get caught up in the finer details, then chances are you are dealing with a C-style person.

The late Steve Jobs, a man known for his attention to detail and the chief executive of Apple Corp, was a master of this. For him, no stone was left unturned in his quest for perfection in the products that Apple manufacture. Famed for his eye for detail and being obsessive about the customer experience, everything had to look right to him even if it wasn't that noticeable to others. One example of this is with the pixelation on a computer screen. Leander Kahney[3] mentions in his book *Inside Steve's Brain* how he used to get his face close up to the screen to ensure that the pixels of the screen looked right. The vast majority of the population wouldn't consider such a detail, but Steve did.

The C-style is always looking for reasoning and is focused mainly on the 'why'? They want to understand the workings of everything and how things fit together. If something doesn't look right, you can

---

[3]   Kahney, L. (2008), *Inside Steve's Brain* (Portfolio Hardcover)

be sure that the C-style personality will want to understand why. I was managing a financial accountant and we were going through a set of numbers together. After spotting that something just didn't look right we then went about trying to resolve what it was. It wasn't a significant or material amount that we were looking for. After going through many avenues to solve it, I decided to work on something else and thought we'd figure it out later after a break. My colleague, however, wasn't satisfied with this and wanted to resolve it there and then. He worked until 11 p.m. that evening trying to get to the bottom of it, and he did.

Alex Ferguson, the ex-manager of the English football team Manchester United, used to manage his team with an iron fist. He was famed for his 'hair-dryer' treatment of players who stepped out of line or who didn't perform as well as they could have. He undoubtedly has a D-style. However, it was left for Carlos Quieroz, who used to work as Alex's second in command and is a C-style, to ensure that what Alex wanted from his players was carried out on the training ground and, ultimately, on the football pitch. Quieroz's tactfulness as well as his eye for detail complemented Ferguson's more direct style of management.

> *No matter how smart you are you need a team of great people. You've got to figure out how to size people up quickly and hire them. And then once you have hired them, let them develop in a way that complements their strengths.*

Indirect Style

One of the traits of the C-style personality is their ability to stay objective which enables them to remain impassive to their environment. They keep a cool head and let the data or facts do the talking which can be an invaluable skill to have in certain professions like accountancy and medicine. They can take an emotive subject and put it into context, which can take the heat out of a difficult situation.

During three seasons of frantic transfer speculation, one of the most eagerly awaited soccer transfers in Europe finally happened.

It concluded with the biggest transfer fee of any one single player in the history of the game. In 2009, the sale of Cristiano Ronaldo for £80 million to Real Madrid from Manchester United dominated the papers and people from all sides were expressing their views. One was Carlos Quieroz who used to manage the player when he was at United. He had this to say when the question of loyalty came up between player and team.

'When you talk about loyalty, you must understand the loyalty has two directions... In terms of the modern game, loyalty is to be a great professional, to be committed to the club, to be engaged with the coach and the vision of the club and nobody can put one thing against Cristiano because as a professional he's brilliant. But as you know with 95 per cent or 96 per cent of movement in football it is the managers at the clubs that dictate the movements. Once in a while some of the top players have the capacity and the power to create their own motivation.'[4]

The ability to put things into context through the clever use of pragmatic language supported with clear examples is what C-styles do very well.

Task-oriented

Doing the right things right

The C-style is quite a task-oriented person. While not as bottom-line focused as the D-style, they are both equally focused on the task at hand. For the C-style, everything has its rightful place. With an appetite for detail, they place more importance on this than just getting things done.

They like certainty and having things just right gives them peace of mind. To this end, they also like to have structure as this ensures a reliable result. If a structure isn't in place, the C-style will ask why and then proceed to put one in place.

---

[4] *The Telegraph* online article: http://www.telegraph.co.uk/sport/football/teams/manchester-united/5531842/Cristiano-Ronaldo-transfer-Manchester-United-winger-brilliant-professional.html

Critically-minded, new ideas will be subject to a raft of questions from the C-style personality. Where the I-style might naturally get excited about a business idea that sounds great, the C-style will treat it with caution and will want to pore over certain facts and figures before proceeding.

C-style people are concerned with the quality of the product and they will keep going until it is as they specifically want it. The D-style, on the other hand, is mainly concerned with getting it done. This focus of the C-style on getting it right can cause problems. Others will often perceive them as going too far in the pursuit of perfection. Not everyone is going to be comfortable checking and re-checking and this can affect working relationships.

Whilst DISC has four main categories (D, I, S and C), it doesn't mean to say we are exclusively any one or any two or any three of these categories. From the outset, it is important to acknowledge that we are all four types. Whether this be through nature or nurture, the degree of intensity of each type differs depending on the environment; this is what makes us unique and at the same time brings with it an element of predictability to our behaviour.

Tip: DISC in numbers

D-style: 1+1 = '*Whatever I want it to be!*'
I-style: 1+1 = '*I just love your tie, where did you get it from? What was the question again?*'
S-style: 1+1 = '*Sorry, are you asking me?*'
C-style: 1+1 = '*... 2*' (after some deep thought)

When we wake up in the morning, we each follow a routine to prepare for the rest of the day. For instance, some of us prefer to snooze and some get out of bed instantly. I like to wake up slowly and hit the snooze button about three times at ten-minute intervals before I get out of bed. I have friends who get up as soon as the alarm rings. My pattern of waking up has been developed over a period of time and although there may be times when I need to get up instantly, I prefer to wake up in my own time. In short, I have a waking pattern. We all have our patterns for waking, eating, sleeping, working, being with family etc. People are creatures of habit after all, habits make our lives easier.

Ultimately, the four DISC sections are like a guitar. The guitar only has six strings but can play so many tunes. Depending on where you depress each string, you'll get a different sound. And for each song, every string will be used to a certain degree. People are no different. People play out different situations using certain DISC combinations even though we tend to have a preferred dominant style most of the time.

You may have recognised some behaviour types in the four descriptions outlined in this chapter. You may have recognised some that are relevant to you and some that are relevant to others. This will be a common theme throughout this book and what I'd suggest is to keep an open mind about the possibilities. Sometimes we are quick to jump to conclusions about what we, ourselves, are about and this could hamper your learning.

Summary

D-style (Direct + Task)

The D-style is the personality that focuses on the bottom line. They are concerned with results and usually concentrate on getting things done. Tell them they can't do something and they'll find a way to prove you wrong, such is their level of confidence. Here are some descriptions of a D-style:

- Doesn't like rules. Would prefer to make their own.
- Focused on the bottom line.
- Can be demanding in style and wants things yesterday.
- They are Direct in their style of communication.
- They are resilient and if one way doesn't work, they will find another way.

I-style (Direct + People)

The I-style personality also has confidence in their ability, although it is especially high when it comes to interacting with others.

33

People-oriented, the I-style is the entertainer who is comfortable being the centre of attention. Descriptions of this style include:

- You will usually find this person on the phone or with other people.
- Good at networking.
- Enjoys social activities.
- Has a very cheery disposition and sees the positive side of things.
- Full of enthusiasm and can inspire others to do things through their powers of influence.

S-style (Indirect + People)

Quiet and unassuming, this style prefers to join in with team activities and is more than willing for the I-style or others to take the limelight. They would rather stay in the background and focus on the things that they need to. A team-player, the S-style is someone people tend to trust as they are very good listeners and look out for their friends and acquaintances. Other traits of this style include:

- Reliable, you can depend on them.
- They are not the loudest of people but do speak more when they are comfortable in their surroundings.
- They care about others and what is happening in their lives.
- Tend to shy away from conflict and if they disagree, would rather not speak out unless they have to.
- Prefer to maintain the status quo than take a risk on something with an uncertain outcome.

C-style (Indirect + Task)

Finally, you have the C-style, who is the fountain of all knowledge. Detail-oriented, this type likes to have all things in their rightful place and organisation is their forte. They like to have all the facts when making a decision and want to know everything about everything. Descriptions include:

- Want something analysed, then this style is great at that.
- Perfectionists, they will always find something wrong, so pleasing this type can be difficult.
- They tend to be the deep thinkers of the four DISC types.
- C-styles like to plan ahead.
- They focus on quality and precision.

Chapter 3

Why is the DISC tool important?

'Insanity: doing the same thing over and over again and
expecting different results'
Albert Einstein

When we get up in the morning, we have our personal rituals which are automatic: some of us snooze and some of us get up instantly. Such patterns aren't just restricted to mornings but are common throughout our daily lives. In certain instances, we will behave in particular ways and the more we behave in these ways the more they become habitual to us.

A manager who has a C-style working on a project is likely to want some form of structure, to get the details behind it. For a similar project, the I-style person would want to get everyone involved with the project together so that they can have a discussion and assign roles. This meeting may end with some people knowing roughly what their tasks are, and to the I-style manager, this is progress. To the C-style manager, however, the project plan must be written down and everyone must know exactly how they are doing against a given timeframe. Either way, the same project is managed in two different ways because these two types of people see things differently.

The Input/Output DISC-filter Cycle

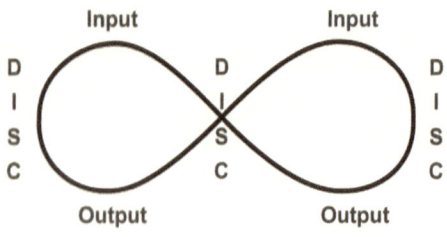

Fig. 3.1 The Input/Output DISC-filter cycle

Figure 3.1 shows how DISC impacts all types of communication. Whether we are receiving or passing on information, it will inevitably be influenced by our own DISC style. This is called the DISC-filter cycle due to the theory that whatever it is, we filter information according to our DISC style. Whether we want to see the details or the bottom-line, this is due to our DISC behavioural style.

The best starting place you have is YOU! And one of the reasons why this is so is because we all have our own perspective (your perspective) on any given situation. In NLP (Neuro Linguistic Programming) this is more commonly referred to as your 'map-of-the-world'. This states that two people can see the same image and will each describe it differently to each other, highlighting different things. Our own personal filters, which are built up through our experiences, learning, education etc form a unique perspective from which we see the world.

> *'First Seek to Understand, then to be Understood.'*
> Stephen Covey

As a result, when we understand where our natural inclinations are (our DISC style), we can understand what our preferences and anxieties are. For example, the C-style will tend to get frustrated with the lack of attention to detail that the I-style shows in their work. However, if the C-style understood their own preference for detail, then their expectations of others could be managed better. They could begin to understand that not everyone will prefer detail and, therefore, manage their own expectations of the other person.

The Input/Output process is a diagram highlighting how the communication cycle works and how DISC plays a central role in this. Although DISC is at the centre of the process, the real work actually starts at the input stage. What is inputted (the message) and how it is inputted gets processed and the output is the feedback of this process. The output then forms the input of the next level and so on and so forth. Just like when someone juggles!

Input here can be anything that is fed into the system. The input could be the question that is asked by you when you are getting to know the person. The response that you receive is the output, and this output is a result of the other person's thought process, which is where DISC comes in. Because it is in a continuous flow (like in a conversation), this process is never-ending as we are constantly communicating for information.

DISC in this diagram works as a filter because the message that comes to us is filtered by our own thoughts and then our own response is constructed through this.

What Figure 3.1 also highlights is that with ourselves and the recipients, our filters are always there and the skill comes in understanding which filters, or DISC style, the other person prefers, so that we can then appreciate the world in the way that they see it. The more we understand our own style preference, the more we are able to appreciate that of someone else, as our own style can be used as a benchmark against theirs.

One of the main elements of the DISC Cycle is the Input element. Whatever you put in you are going to get out. So if you don't ask the right question you are not going to get the right answer. We, therefore, have to be extra vigilant and patient with the other person. We have to learn to listen and observe as the DISC style they prefer is going to be evident in the responses they give.

Continuous improvement with the DISC Cycle

No right or wrong answer

Whether we like it or not, it is easy to judge others. Our minds cannot help but think. One of the benefits of DISC is that we begin to understand people from how they behave. To a certain degree we put ourselves in a position where we can ascertain the style of someone else's behaviour; and because we can now put a perspective on this behaviour, it just becomes another way of behaving. When we see it this way, we are able to see behaviour for what it is, surface level, so judgement can be put into perspective as we observe and take in what we see. It would be good to be able to do this with ourselves also. There is no right or wrong way of behaving, just that we have chosen to behave in the way we have. Your behaviour is your behaviour and right now we want to understand where we are.

Progress is not linear

One of the wonderful things about ball games is that no matter how good you are, you will always end up having a bad day somewhere along the line. When I began to play golf, I remember my progress was really slow. Then one day it all came together. I found myself striking the ball beautifully and was really excited by this development. I remember going home and dreaming of the shots I had played and also visualising the ones I was going to play next time I was on the course. The next day came, with my confidence high, and I was desperate to get back onto the course. When I eventually did I played a terrible game. It wasn't that I played badly at all, it was that my expectations of how I would play were very high. Unreal almost. I took one good game as proof that this is the standard I can maintain from this point on. But it doesn't work that way. Sometimes as one part of the game improves, another element falls by the wayside. A bit like a Rubik's cube, when you have completed one whole side, if you want to complete all the other sides, you inevitably end up breaking up that one completed side. I started to analyse my golf game and had to change the style I had naturally developed. As I began to make conscious changes, my game at times showed progress whilst also signs of falling to pieces. I had to keep the faith as I knew my game would keep improving if I just kept at it. Failure, as they say, only happens when you quit. Keeping at it and learning from your errors ensures it's a continuous process and a never-ending journey of learning.

We all learn in different ways so it is important to appreciate that DISC can only help you understand a certain amount of someone's behaviour. Sometimes, like we all do, someone will just get out of the wrong side of the bed and have one of those days that they would rather forget. Stick to learning the various behaviour styles and learn to play around with them. Although we are predictably different, it can be the unpredictable that makes things more interesting. Obviously, that is me, the I-style side, speaking. For the S-style and C-style, seeing it this way may not necessarily be so easy.

Celebrate, not tolerate

Part of putting ourselves into the position of others is that with this empathy we start to see things the way they see things. At times, it's easy to get so caught up in our train of thought that if anything conflicts with what we are currently seeing we consider it an annoyance. However, if we sat back for a second and listened to what the other person had to say, maybe we would find something valuable in what they are saying for example, something that would save us time, money and effort.

The 'throw' is where everything begins. There is a saying in tennis that goes 'the ball is in your court'. Because you now have this ball, it is up to you what to do with it. In communication, when someone is speaking, you have control over whether to make yourself present for them or not and whether you want to listen to what they have to say. So how you receive their message will also depend on the mindset that you are currently in. Are you being receptive or sceptical or pessimistic? On the whole, our mindset is often whatever we want it to be.

By tolerating a person, we are coming from a place of doing them a favour and this is not generally an empowering place to come from. Adults do this to children a lot. We may hear but don't really listen to what they are saying and some of us may find ourselves only going through the motions of listening. However, by doing this, we are closing ourselves off from wisdom that they are sharing with us. We are turning away from the opportunity of getting to know them better and understanding how they see the world.

If, on the other hand, we learned to celebrate rather than tolerate then we could change our whole attitude to how we receive the other person. We would begin from the outset of being more receptive to them, to what they are saying, how they are saying it and what they really mean.

The other person's motivations

If someone doesn't want to do something, they simply won't do it.

No one can really get you to do something if you don't have the motivation to do it. What one can do, however, is to create the environment for people to prosper and to take action for themselves. Motivation is innate and if we can create a supportive environment for them to take action, then you won't have to do much but guide the person.

I used to have this terrible habit of biting my nails which started way back in my childhood. Up until the age of about 25, biting my nails was habitual. My mother was so incensed at such a bad habit she tried many things to discourage me, but to no avail. Although I knew biting my nails wasn't the greatest thing to do, I just kept on doing it thinking it would be extremely difficult to stop. However, I then heard this story in a seminar which resonated with me and the result was instant.

The presenter relayed a story of how he couldn't understand this girl sitting opposite him on the train who constantly bit her nails. He mentioned that not only did her nails look 'scabby' but there were also some serious 'hygiene problems going on'. He explained how some people go to the toilet and don't wash their hands and that these same people then go on to use the same public facilities as everyone else, like pushing the buttons of a lift or holding onto the side of an escalator or just simply opening doors etc. However, no matter how much we wash our hands, the dirt underneath our fingernails was more difficult to remove. Then people like the girl opposite him on the train would put those germs straight into their mouths when they bit their nails. 'Why would anyone willingly want to do that?' he asked us.

This story touched a chord and I stopped biting my nails almost instantly. What the presenter had done was enter my 'map of the world' and, by relaying the story, got me to make the choice of whether I wanted to bite my nails or not. I didn't feel I had many choices as there was really only one logical thing to do—stop biting my nails! And so I did.

Because he tapped into my motivation, I was able to take action for myself without him directly asking me to do so. This is also what a manager is doing when they create the environment in which his/

her team members can prosper. Build a supportive environment and watch your people take the steps.

Summary

Be mindful of who you are going to interact with. Customising your message to a style that they are more receptive to will increase your chances of coming across more effectively. This requires you to be aware of your own style so that you can adjust towards someone else's.

Other things to be mindful of include:

No right and wrong answer: We all have our own styles and no style is better or worse than another. Yes, it may be appropriate to behave in a certain way depending on the situation, and in doing so, adapting your own style to accommodate for this but a style is just a style.

Progress is not linear: Keep at it. You are the way you are through a combination of nature and nurture. More importantly, your habits have been formed over time. So adopting a different approach to something that you would do naturally will take time to get used to. One day you may think things have started to fall into place and then the next day you think otherwise. Don't despair, take the learnings and keep at it.

Celebrate not tolerate: Being receptive to someone else's style can only help us in getting to understand them better, thereby putting us in a position of learning and empowerment.

Chapter 4

Playing to your strengths

We all have our strengths and weaknesses. In society, we have learned to focus more on our weaknesses—and on the air-brushed images on the billboards, our TV screens and at the cinema. Whatever it is, we have been conditioned to focus on what we lack. In a poll conducted by Marcus Buckingham[5] he asked parents which of the following grades they would spend the most time discussing with their son or daughter:

A - English
A - Social Studies
C - Biology
F - Algebra

He found that an astonishing 77% of parents chose to spend the majority of their time focusing on the F in Algebra. Only 6% chose to focus on the A in English and even less, 1%, chose to spend more time on the A in social studies.

A past president of the American Psychological Association, Martin Seligman, reported that he found over 40,000 articles on the subject of depression and only 40 on the subject of joy, happiness or fulfilment. He wasn't saying that depression isn't something to be studied as it is a serious illness that is growing by the day—he was highlighting how skewed research was towards one side. 'Psychology is half-baked, literally half-baked. We have baked the part about mental illness. We have baked the part about repair and damage. But the other side is unbaked. The side of strengths, the side of what we are good at, the side… of what makes life worth living.'

---

[5]   Buckingham, M., Clifton, D.O. (2005), *Now, discover your strengths,* Pocket Books http://gmj.gallup.com/content/559/are-you-afraid-of-your-weaknesses.aspx)

> *'When we focus on our strengths, we can learn to see*
> *others for theirs'*
> Zahoor Bargir

Whatever the reasons for focusing on our weaknesses, to do this at the detriment of our strengths is an injustice we are committing against ourselves and those around us. Why do I mention this? Well, when we work on our strengths we can learn to see others for theirs. When we see others for their strengths, we are able to reach greater possibilities, as others will be more willing to support us by making an even bigger contribution. The energy levels increase and you have greater activity in the right direction under better leadership.

Someone's strengths can be described as their most natural state. Some call this talent, as it could be something they are inherently good at and find relatively easy to do. When we are playing to our strengths, things come easier to us. We find more enjoyment in what we do and are even more willing to go that extra mile whenever required to do so.

It's in our moment of strength, of pure focus, when we find ourselves in 'the zone'. That illusive place where we are at one with what we are doing, where everything else falls by the wayside, where our focus is purely on the task at hand. This is not to say that we shouldn't work on our weaknesses, but more that we should learn to focus more on our strengths.

Strengths of the D-style

The television programme, *The Apprentice* (in the UK) is headed by Lord Sugar (who has a D-style) and he has his two trusted advisors who have complementary styles. Can you imagine all three being like Lord Sugar—THREE D-styles? It would be havoc with so many egos vying for control in one place and we would no doubt be more entertained by the three D-styles in action than with the competitors.

If an organisation requires shaking up, the D-style is the natural choice to get things happening. With their resilience and straightforward demeanour, tasks which other styles may find difficult the D-style will enjoy. Here are some of the main advantages of having the D-style in your team.

Goal-oriented, when a team is being led by a D-style, there is no hesitation in which direction it is heading. D-style personalities are likely to shake a team up if it isn't achieving what it should be achieving, and in their own direct style, everyone will get to know about it. Being bottom-line focused, nothing but what the team is aiming for is going to be good enough. They'll likely question what everyone is doing and if they don't find a viable reason for every person being in the team, the D-style will see to it that they either find something more relevant to do or ply their services elsewhere.

Being thick-skinned, at a time when change needs to happen immediately, the D-style is the one to make the change happen. They are not that susceptible to what other people think and if it is the right thing to do, they will take action, even if it is likely to make them unpopular.

Their natural drive and persistence allows them to shake up slow-moving systems. Through their strategic outlook and powerful personality, they get things moving a lot quicker than the other styles.

The addition of a D-style to an established team can have both positive and negative consequences. A positive impact could be that a team that may have been 'coasting' will be galvanised into action again, when they could, quite easily, have lost their edge. On the negative side, a team that has achieved a good balance and a solid state of coherence can find that balance affected by this new imposing figure that has joined the team, and is intent on changing a few things.

D-styles are generally good problem solvers. Their strength in seeing the woods from the trees allows them to sift through information very quickly. Their incredible mental capacity and confidence allows them to take in and process complex information. This allows them to go right to the heart of the problem. While others may get caught up in detail or fail to find a way through much conflicting information, their pragmatism allows them to marry theory with practice to come up with a viable solution to a problem.

D-styles like to keep things simple. Although they are more than capable of handling complexity, they prefer simplicity as it saves them time. Time is the essence for the D-style as they have usually got their fingers in many pies. So anything that helps them save time is a major plus.

Their decisiveness, especially in times of need, can be a real blessing when the team is looking for inspiration from somewhere. It also allows momentum to follow in a certain direction which may otherwise have been lost if indecision had been allowed to set in.

They are more than capable of dealing with numerous projects at the same time. Because they have the skill of getting to the heart of something quickly the D-style can make maximum use of their talents.

D-style—When strengths become weaknesses

As the saying goes, 'too much of a good thing can be bad for you'. And often, good qualities and strengths can become weaknesses if overdone.

Confidence > Arrogance

Confidence is a key attribute when doing anything and the D-style usually has it in abundance. Not shy to express their point of view, when they say things it is usually said with certainty and confidence. Confidence can instil a can-do feeling in others who are then inspired to be more motivated to take action. However, arrogance, which is closer to over-confidence, may have the opposite effect and turn people away from being inspired. Instead of people wanting to work with you and be around you, they may be less inclined to contribute (except out of fear maybe) and are less happy to be around such a person. One way confidence can come out in the right way is for the D-style to be encouraged to listen. Listening to what others have to say and allowing team members to speak up gives them a sense of contribution and being a part of something.

Being more social beings, I- and S-styles may view the confidence of D-styles as a good thing, especially when taken in the context of getting things done. However, both may also see the actions of the D-style, at times, as lacking compassion. So whilst the workplace is a place to get things done, relationships and feelings play a big part in how they operate. With the D-style and their focus on the task, both I- and S-styles may find this way of working impersonal and unfriendly. Over-confidence would make it feel more so, and could affect their team morale.

The C-style, on the other hand, may see the D-style's confidence as superficial until they have seen results to confirm that there is substance to back it up. The C-style may also find that the D-style goes too fast as they tend to work at their own pace and expect everyone else to keep up. In this way, the C-style may just carry on as they are, knowing what they have to do regardless of what the D-style is doing.

Decision maker > Dictator

One of the strengths of a D-style is that they are not afraid of making a decision. This style tends to make a decision based on the facts available to them and proceeds quickly. However, if decisions are constantly made swiftly without consulting others or ignoring what others have to say, this could have an adverse effect on the group. If you have a D-style in your team, get an understanding and agreement with them as to what kind of decisions they can act upon on their own and which they need to seek your counsel on. Getting them to show you how they came to their decision allows you to have confidence in what they have done, whilst allowing the D-style freedom to work on their own initiative.

Multi-tasking > Taking on too much

D-styles are notorious for having many balls up in the air and juggling between one task and another. Their ability to keep an eye on many balls is uncanny and it's a real talent of theirs. However, one thing that could catch them out is if they take on too much and reach breaking point. This is when they could quite easily just drop all the balls and walk away. Saying 'no' to things that come their way, especially when they have too much going on anyway, is a skill they should learn to master.

Strengths of the I-style

Ever need a promoter? Then you don't need to look any further than an I-style. Here are some strengths of the I-style.

The I-style is the inspirational type of the four styles. This type can sell ice to the Eskimos. If you feel the need to be inspired, the I-style is the person to go to. With their high-tempo speech patterns and overall positive outlook on life, they exude confidence. This person is always good to have on a team to keep the energy up and especially so when the rest of the team are in need of inspiration.

Warm and personable, I-styles feel good when they are connecting with others. In a team, this type is the one to get everyone talking and socialising with each other. I remember at one of my previous workplaces, my team of five had two who were I-style dominant. We went against the natural grain of most Finance departments (which are usually more inclined to include C-styles) and began organising lunches and evenings out with the other departments in the organisation. Before the two I-styles joined the Finance team, cross-departmental lunches were not something that commonly happened.

The I-style is full of ideas. Being a dreamer, they may sometimes have trouble following up with concrete action. But ask them for contributions towards an idea, and this type are great at coming up with new ways of doing things or developing existing ideas. For blue-sky thinking, the I-style is in his/her element.

They tend to have a glass half-full attitude to life. The I-style is a master at reframing a situation and seeing the positives. This attitude can be especially important when an organisation is going through periods of change and uncertainty, and when the atmosphere can generally be low.

Being skilled networkers, I-styles are the ones known by everyone in an organisation. Whether it is the mailman, cleaners, managers, analysts... I-styles have a way of connecting to others with ease. One interaction is usually enough for them (and you!) to come away with a new acquaintance. Utilise this skill in an external network setting, and new business opportunities can open up for you quite easily.

Taking this further, they usually also know someone who knows someone. Their list of connections knows no bounds, so if you are searching for a person with a specific set of skills, they'll either know someone or know how to get to the person you want.

I-styles have a creative mindset. They are especially good at making connections where you may have thought there weren't any. Using their creativity, they can show you how to achieve something with what you've already got. So if resources are short, whether it is labour, money, time etc, the I-style can find a way of getting round such a situation. Just like an ant, if they don't get to where they want one way they'll figure out another way until they do.

They can be behaviourally quite expressive and emotional. So whilst they may show emotion a lot sooner, than say an S-style or a C-style, they are also more able to recover from disappointment a lot quicker as well. Their power of recovery is one of their strong points, and something the S- and C-styles can learn from.

If you need someone to present a pitch, the I-style can be a brilliant candidate. If they can stick to the job at hand and not get too carried away with being in the limelight, they are able to connect easily with the audience with their affable and easy-going style. They may suffer nerves just like everyone else, but with their natural confidence in front of others they are able to come across positively to the audience.

I-style—When strengths become weaknesses

New ideas > Incomplete work

One of the strengths of the I-style is their ability to dream and think up new ideas. However, this creativity takes another slant when the ideas are generated but nothing comes of them. I-style personalities can be working on one thing, and then they get inspired and move off into another direction, leaving what they were working on unfinished. This can get really frustrating for other team members. Scheduling completion dates will enable the I-style to focus on their timetable and ensure things are done when they need to be done.

Unstructured way of working > Poor attention to detail

One of the strengths of the I-style is their way of creating something out of nothing. When they make decisions, they can take in many angles of a problem and make a decision which they feel is best suited to a situation. This is especially the case when it comes to working with people and considering their needs, the I-style has a knack of empathising with others and seeing things from their perspective and working out a win/win situation. However, for work that requires attention to detail, their less-than-structured way of working can be a big shortcoming as they can be prone to miss out important details in their work. This lack of consistency in how they operate can be really frustrating to teammates, especially to the C-style.

Good communicator > Poor time-planner

The I-style tends to be a confident communicator. When it comes to talking, they are not shy and can really make the person they are working with feel great about the task at hand and the things to do. However, it's not uncommon for the I-style to agree to something and then fail to put it into their calendar (if they have one), ending up with conflicting schedules or finding they've taken on too much. Better organisation would enable them to work at a more leisurely and less stressful pace.

Quick decisions > Incomplete decision-making

Where the D-style is able to make quick decisions, so can the I-style. Led by instinct, this can be a useful tool whenever the situation requires. However, making decisions based on instinct or feelings can also be counterproductive if facts and figures that are available are disregarded. Analysing the data that is available would enable the I-style person to come to a more informed decision. Suffice to say, the C-style person finds it very difficult to work with the I-style as one is purely fact-focused whereas the other is more adept at coming to decisions based on instinct.

Strengths of the S-style

'Don't leave home without it.' This is what you could say about the S-style—they are the people who get what you want done.

Reliable and consistent, team members know what they are getting with the S-style. They can be relied upon to produce the work when it is needed, once they have carried out the task a few times. In this way, they are comfortable with work requiring repetition whilst also maintaining a certain level of quality. This enables them to be dependable team members.

Orderly and efficient, the S-style likes to keep things simple in their immediate surroundings. This makes it easier for others to follow what they are doing as they'll have a functional way of operating. So when an S-style manager wants to delegate a piece of work, it'll most likely be documented and easier to take on.

The S-style person is a strong team player. Naturally empathetic, they are in touch with others around them and can relate with them on more than just a professional level. Because of this, although they aren't as overtly friendly as the I-style, they are still able to connect with people on a deeper level and build strong, meaningful relationships. In the context of a change programme, they provide a shoulder to cry on as well as bringing stability to a strenuous situation. However, they are the first to get nervous during a change situation, so to get the best out of them at such a time, try to keep them in the loop with what is going on and be reassuring. They don't like surprises (work that comes in at the last minute) or anything that takes them outside their comfort zone.

With this empathy, members of a team where the manager is an S-style are more likely to feel supported. They will feel like their concerns are being heard and may find that their manager is willing to spend more time with them. So instead of telling them what to do, S-style managers may be more inclined to demonstrate and show them what they are looking for.

With their tendency to be more introverted as well as people-oriented, S-styles can often be misconstrued as more suited to support roles. Not so. With directorship and management roles sometimes being dominated by the more extroverted styles, having S-style managers in the mix often balances out the flavour of the management team. S-style managers can often bring calm and a voice of reason to discussions and decision-making. They are also likely to be more in touch with the rest of the people in the organisation and, therefore, better at representing those who aren't there.

Because they tend to be more unassuming, and have an easy-going manner, S-styles are like the 'glue' of a team in an organisation. They may not be as vocal as their D- and I-style counterparts, but when they aren't there that's when you realise the true contribution that they make.

This style is inclined to put the team first, before their own interests. They tend not to be so interested in making a big name for themselves, as pulling their weight for the betterment of the team. This makes them flexible to taking on roles that are needed for the benefit of the team. And often, these roles could include non-prestigious ones that people don't want to take on. Due to their flexibility, they can be quite influential within the team from whatever position they are in.

They are extremely good listeners. Rising above the notion of wanting to stand out from the crowd, the S-style is likely to sit back and listen to all the views being put forward. If the team comes up with ideas and agrees through consensus what course of action to take, the S-style is willing to go along with what has been agreed. Having heard what has been discussed and said, they won't necessarily step forward and volunteer what they think unless otherwise asked to do so. Although it can sometimes be to their own detriment that they don't speak up, bringing them into the conversation from the sidelines can be beneficial as they often will have heard what everyone has had to say before giving an opinion.

S-style—When strengths become weaknesses

Team first > Unwilling to take initiative

The S-style is one that likes to put the team first. They see themselves as team players and do whatever is needed for the good of the team. However, taken to an extreme, the S-style can become too reactive. Consequently, they may be unwilling to take the initiative when the time is right to do so.

Good at doing what's asked > Miss the bigger picture

You can always rely on the S-style to produce consistently good work. If you ask them to do something, if they know what they are doing, you can be sure they'll produce the goods. Sometimes, however, they can become so dependent on working to instructions that they fail to think things through properly for themselves. Getting them to see and think of the bigger picture might help them to think things through a little more. This will enable them to see how different things impact each other as opposed to seeing things in a more abstract fashion.

Consistent and process-oriented > Unable to find a better way of doing things

One of the strengths of the S-style is their consistency. Once they have mastered how to do something, they are usually very good at churning out work of a similar quality, consistently. However, one of the downsides to this is sometimes they get so comfortable doing something in a regular fashion, they want to stay in this gear and not look for ways of improving the current process. Change is something they are not comfortable with, therefore, they do need time and encouragement, in a friendly way, to find better ways of doing something. After all, they are usually the ones who are working hard where it matters, on the shopfloor.

Strengths of the C-style

The C-style is the thinker of the four styles. Slow and methodical, they won't let something pass until they have got to the bottom of the problem. Quality is defined by this style. While others may be satisfied at the quality of work achieved, the C-style people are the ones to take it to the next level. Like the other styles, here are some strengths of this style.

Give them an intellectual challenge and they'll thrive. They like nothing more than to get their head down and try to figure something out. They will not only want to see that something adds up, but they'll also want to see that it makes sense. If you want a thorough job done, give it to the C-style person.

Being the thinker, they are constantly looking for a better way. The term 'continuous improvement', which was made famous by the Quality Circle fraternity, probably had this style in mind when they came up with it. In fact, it was probably this style that thought it up in the first instance. When I was consulting, one of the first challenges at a client's office was to re-engineer how one whole department was run. Being pushed for time and under-resourced, we got help from many quarters so Linda (a Personal Assistant to a company partner) in another department came to help out. Being adept at operating the software, she worked on developing the flowcharts which were already part drawn-up etc. The flowcharts began to display enormous amounts of detail which drew everyone's attention. Suffice to say, Linda became a permanent fixture on the consulting team, eventually becoming a senior member of the project going forward.

The inquisitive mind: If you ever want to see how something is broken down, give it to a C-style. Taking something big and breaking it down into bitesize chunks is an art in itself. It requires an inquisitive and patient mind, someone who isn't satisfied with how things are and is willing to break things up for the sake of knowing how it was put together.

This style is also an editor. Due to their penchant for detail, you can always rely on them to spot things others haven't picked up. Give the task of checking a piece of work to a C-style and you can be sure they will pick up things that have been missed. They will pick up every nuance in your piece. The D-style won't even have the patience of going through such an arduous task.

Completing a piece of work is also an art. It's always easier starting something than finishing it off, which requires much patience and energy. By their very nature, C-styles want to finish what they have started. Give them something mid-way, and they'll go right to the beginning and work their way up to where you are now and continue from there. It can be a thankless task with many people losing interest once the initial euphoria of getting a project up and running has passed, but the C-style person will keep going until all loose ends are tied up. Every good team needs people who can make sure others see the task is completed to the end. Therefore, C-styles are invaluable to any team.

The ability to think ahead and to anticipate obstacles is an area in which this type is also quite adept. Their penchant for thinking ahead and planning so that nothing is overlooked is second to none. They are consistent in their approach and can often spot some problem further along the line, even before it has surfaced. The capacity to do this requires thinking through eventual possibilities and matching them with probabilities. C-style thinkers can save you many headaches by looking at contingency strategies.

C-style—When strengths become weaknesses

Analytical > Paralysis by over-analysis

One strength of a C-style is being able to see a situation from many different angles and then coming to a decision based on having all the facts. Put to an extreme, it isn't uncommon for the C-style to over-do it and hold up on making a decision due to thinking they haven't got enough information. Not wanting to make a wrong decision, the danger lies in overcomplicating a situation so much that they put themselves into a confused state as well as everybody else around them.

Perfection > Not enough time

You would find it difficult to fault the work of the C-style person. Their pursuit for perfection is legendary. In the meantime, time is ticking away with a deadline looming and still the C-style isn't close to finishing as they have spent way too much time on one part of the project which has left them with little time to focus on other areas.

High quality work > Prioritising becomes a problem

The C-style person tends to place a premium on producing work which is of a high quality. For the C-style, it really is 'if you do anything, you do it properly or don't do it at all'. This can have its problems, however. Some things don't necessarily need the required attention that the C-style would give. Spending too much time in one area can have a knock-on effect in other areas. Is it any wonder they may feel overwhelmed at times with the amount they have to do?

High opinion of themselves > Too judgemental/critical

When it comes to quality, the C-style person knows their stuff. They'll be the one who will painstakingly go through the detail to ensure everything is correct and looks absolutely perfect, whether it is how something looks or making sure everything adds up. Because they spend much time on the finer details, it's not unusual for them to expect this of others too. While this may up the quality of work others produce, they may eventually get discouraged to do it at all, thinking 'what's the point when it is never good enough anyway?'

Systemisation > Takes away the human and fun element of working

The C-style just loves to have a system in place for their work. The facts must speak for themselves as the human element is what the C-style tries to minimise. They prefer to see human interaction in a system minimised (or eliminated altogether) as humans are 'usually the cause of errors'. To the C-style, the workplace is for doing purely this—working. The human side, however, is what the I-style and the S-style place a high value on. They see the workplace as a place to meet and interact with others, the people they work with have a big impact on whether they enjoy their work or not. Taken too far, the C-style may take away the fun of working for others who value different things.

Summary

D-style strengths

- Good decision-makers, especially when a decision is needed with minimal information.
- Willing to take on responsibility.
- They are resilient and like to learn the lesson and move on.
- Not afraid to make tough decisions and stand their ground.
- Good at problem solving and fire-fighting.
- Efficient and productive workers especially when it comes to saving time and money.

D-style weaknesses

- Over-confidence can sometimes come across as being brash and arrogant.
- Can jump in head-first sometimes, when a more considered approach would have been the favoured option.
- Can be too task-oriented, at the expense of team morale and team building.
- Tendency to highlight what went wrong very quickly, while good work can be taken as a given, with praise being in short supply.
- Can have a tendency to take on too much work.

I-style strengths

- I-styles can be fun and inspiring to have around, especially with their jovial nature.
- Able to work in an unstructured way, if the environment is conducive to it.
- Being people-oriented, they can think in terms of the customer and what the customer would like.
- Their strong people skills make them natural networkers, building relationships quickly.
- They can be creative and full of new ideas, forever finding new opportunities.

- See things as glass half-full and forever the optimists.
- Good with words so have a strong influential style.

I-style weaknesses

- Can get distracted easily and leave work unfinished.
- Although good at seeing the bigger picture, not great with detailed work.
- Prone to forgetting things, and therefore not always good at following through.
- Can jump too easily into making a decision without ascertaining the full facts.
- Prioritising can be a challenge as they allow themselves to get bogged down by too many opportunities that are presented to them.

S-style strengths

- S-style types are team-players who put the interests of the team first.
- They have an easy-going nature and are good listeners.
- They have a strong focus on getting the job done and are always willing to go the extra mile to ensure the work is done satisfactorily.
- Loyalty is a particularly strong point of theirs, especially when they have built up relationships over a period of time.
- Once they know what to do, you can leave them to it.
- Good with following-through on what needs to be done.

S-style weaknesses

- Making a decision can be a challenge.
- Are unwilling to step forward and be counted, preferring to stay in the background.
- Can at times be too slow in their approach, so in times of urgency, it may take time for them to react to the circumstances.
- More reactive than proactive in their approach, they need help with taking the initiative.

C-style strengths

- Produce work to a very high standard.
- Detail-oriented so you can be sure their work is thorough and fully checked.
- Decision-making is derived after collating all the facts and figures, therefore, little chance of making a hasty decision.
- Ability to stay objective by putting feelings to one side and taking action based on what the situation requires by studying the facts and data.
- They have a disciplined, logical and structured approach to their work which others can follow.
- Good analytical skills which are useful at spotting patterns and trends which can help ascertain future direction.

C-style weaknesses

- Perfectionist streak means producing work on time can on occasions be a challenge.
- Can have a tendency to find decision-making tough if they don't have the full facts at hand.
- Being masters of their craft, in times of urgency, they may not find it easy to submit a piece of work which is 'good enough'. For them, you either do it well or not at all.
- Can be inflexible at times by sticking to the 'right' way, when other ways could be more effective, albeit taking a short cut to get to the objective.
- Take the human element out of the work process, which happens to be a big part of the way of working for the I- and S-styles.

Chapter 5

We all leave clues

It would be good if we could get everyone to take a DISC profile and pass it on to us but that is unlikely to happen. So what we have to go on is what we can observe through their actions and hear in what they have to say. Even their touch can give something away about them. It becomes easier to distinguish certain behaviours when we consciously look for clues. Like anything, the more we practise, and become attuned to seeing different behavioural attributes, the better we become at picking them up.

I once attended a seminar where the speaker said it isn't possible not to communicate and he's absolutely correct. Various studies[6] have shown that the language we use forms about 7% of communication, tonality is about 38% of communication and body language is around 55% of communication. Why is body language such a big part of the communication process? Well, because even before we utter a single word, someone has already formed an opinion of us, whether accurate or not. They have formed this evaluation by looking at our facial expressions or the expressiveness of our body language or likely, both. Even the way we dress gives information about us.

Married couples would say they got to know their spouses better after marriage. When I asked whether there were elements in their spouse's behaviour which gave clues about what they were like before they got married, the majority said YES. They said there were elements of their behaviour that they could have picked up on beforehand, but which only really became clear after they got married. The reason for highlighting this is to show that the clues are always there, but that our skill and willingness to pick up on them determines whether we actually do so or not.

---

[6]   Obtained online from the Body Language expert website: http://www.bodylanguageexpert. co.uk/communication-what-percentage-body-language.html

The more we know what to look out for the better we become at spotting different types. If you tune your senses to watch out for certain behavioural elements, then you'll be better at distinguishing them when you come across them. We will be going over certain questions you can use to help you pick out certain types. I wouldn't say these are exhaustive, and you should certainly develop your own questions for spotting styles in people, but the more questions you have for deciphering someone's behavioural type, the better it is for you in understanding that person.

Finding a way—How to spot a style

Body language

We can usually tell when someone is open or more closed through their body language. Some people have a more relaxed style, a style that shows they are open to communication. When they speak they tend to gesture more with their hands and body. They draw you in when they are speaking or even when they are not and you feel comfortable with this person.

How does the other person use their body? Do they look like they are comfortable with being tactile, or are they more hands-off (-ish) and prefer to keep a distance. Often, we can tell, although there are also cultural influences that can determine how we carry ourselves. We all know someone who embraces the people they know with a big bear hug. They are the life and soul of a party and often we can hear them coming before we see them. They might also be the initiator when greeting someone they don't know. On the other hand, some people prefer to put out their hands and say hello to someone they have just met, but only after they have been approached first.

I remember going to a friend's birthday party at a fairly large restaurant in London. I didn't know any of her friends, and unbeknown to me, she was running very late as she was held up in traffic. I got to the restaurant, walked right past reception and tried looking for her inside but couldn't see her anywhere. I then went back to reception to see if there was a table booked under my friend's name. The receptionist confirmed as much and took me to a table where there must have been about ten people seated. I introduced myself to the group and took a seat. I'm an I-style and felt comfortable doing this. About 45 minutes later, a young lady arrived and sat at our table. I greeted her (with a simple handshake as I didn't know her) and introduced myself. She greeted me with a warm smile, 'Hi, I'm Linda, nice to meet you'. Noticing that her hands were cold, I mentioned this to her (as a typical I-style would). It was then that she told me she'd been waiting in her car for the past hour as our mutual friend was running late. It transpired that Linda didn't want to walk into the restaurant on her own as she didn't know anyone. Both the fact that I initiated contact and that she decided to stay in the car until she was certain she'd know someone at the party suggested an S- or C-style behavioural pattern.

Speech

The way we speak also gives off clues as to our preferred behavioural style. Some people speak very quickly, whereas others like to speak at a slower, more gentle pace. Some people like to say whatever is on their minds. They have a more instinctive way of speaking and words just seem to flow right through them. Others have a more measured way of speaking, and like to think things through before saying anything. Some people seem to have a more 'telling' or direct style of communication whereas others like to ask questions and hold back a little.

The tonality in our speech can also be used to ascertain someone's style preference. The task-oriented styles (D- and C-style) have a more formal, and maybe even direct, tone that seems unwavering, whereas the people-oriented styles (I and S) tend to have more variation in their tones. Their tonality may come across as more friendly with a warm feel.

Surroundings

Our environment can also say a lot about us. The working area of the D-style may not be the tidiest of places but they'll let you know it's their space. The D-style person is someone who likes to make a statement. Proud of their achievements, don't be surprised if they have pictures of themselves or trophies they may have won over the years. Piles of paper, not necessarily in a neat pile, might be on the desk, and the unkempt feel gives the sense of someone in a hurry. And indeed, they almost certainly will be short on time.

Now if you think the D-style's desk is not tidy, you should try seeing the I-style's. Not known for their orderliness, their desk is strewn with paper on and around the desk. Others may find their desk unworkable, but the I-style will know exactly where things are. In fact, tidy it and they'll have more trouble finding their things than when it was messy. Open their desks and it could be even worse. Papers will be stacked on top of each other in no relevant order and often, they'll not be at their desk, or if they are they'll be on the phone.

The more indirect styles tend to have more of a need for order in their immediate surroundings. Take the S-style for instance. Being more people-oriented, they like to have personal mementoes around the office like photos of the family and their friends. They are also more likely to have a warm feeling around their desk space area, somewhere they can personalise and feel comfortable.

Compare this to the clinical work space of the C-style type, with all things neatly stacked and put away in their correct files. They are likely to be the ones who have the full range of stationery neatly tucked away in their desks or somewhere close at hand, leaving clear space for them to work and think. Whereas the S-style might complain about hot-desking, the C-style type wouldn't necessarily mind so much as they might welcome the space and clinical orderliness that hot-desking brings with it.

Through knowing what to look out for, a style is not necessarily as difficult to spot as one may think.

What follows is a structure to deciphering what style someone is employing at a certain moment in time. It is important to remember that this is not a definitive list of things to look out for. You are welcome to add your own questions and use this as a guide to build on.

Questions

For ease of use, the following questions have been divided into two main areas:

Direct/Indirect

and

People/Task

Once you have come to a place where you can identify if a behaviour is one or the other, add up your answers and go with the majority number. Do this for both Direct/Indirect and People/Task areas and see what you get.

Remember: the result that you come up with should only be used as an indicator. It should help you establish a baseline and then work with this to foster a better working relationship. Each person has many facets to them (predictable as they may tend to be) so be open to further learnings as we can all differ in our styles depending on the situation we find ourselves in.

Direct/Indirect:

Focus on what you see and hear.

Decoding the body language of the person:
Open—Expressive body language i.e. in hand gestures, arms etc? [Direct]
Closed—Controlled body language? [Indirect]

Exchanging information:
Have more of a 'telling' style of communication? [Direct]
Ask questions? [Indirect]

Change:
Quick to deal with change? [Direct]
Are they more wary and cautious in reaction to change? [Indirect]

Initial meetings:
Do they make the first move when introducing themselves? [Direct]

Wait for the other person to introduce themselves? [Indirect]

Decision making:
Do they like to make fast decisions? [Direct]
Deliberate over them and take their time? [Indirect]

Environment (i.e. their office):
Cluttered with paper and/or other items? [Direct]
Does this look organised? [Indirect]

Risk:
Take risk in their stride? [Direct]
More risk averse? [Indirect]

The pace of their speech:
Fast? [Direct]
Slow? [Indirect]

Each of these attributes creates the acronym DECIDERS. This can help you remember which attributes to look for.

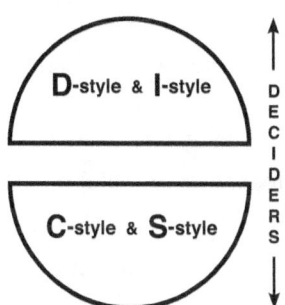

Fig. 5.1 Acronym differentiating between Direct and Indirect

DECIDERS

Decode body language
Exchange information
Change
Initial greeting
Decision making

Environment
Risk
Speech—Pace

Task/People:

Focus on what you see, hear and touch.

Go with the flow:
More willing to go with the flow? [People]
More focused on outcomes and sticks to agenda? [Task]

Orientation: Language and Vocabulary
Concerned more with people and feelings? [People]
Do they use words which are more task/work oriented? [Task]

Their questioning. Are they more concerned with:
Who and How? [People]
What and Why? [Task]

Teamwork. Are they:
Team-oriented? [People]
Prefer to work on own or like to have overall control of the team?
[Task]

Open to:
Expressing their own feelings? [People]
More cautious about opening up? [Task]

Facial Expressions and Body Language:
More expressive? [People]
Gives little away? [Task]

Intonation of Voice:
Varied in pitch? [People]
More formal and to the point? [Task]

Space (Personal). They are:
More comfortable with physical contact? [People]
More protective of their personal space? [Task]

How they make decisions:
They follow their feelings more? [People]
They make decisions in a logical/fact-based way? [Task]

These questions create the acronym GOT TO FISH.

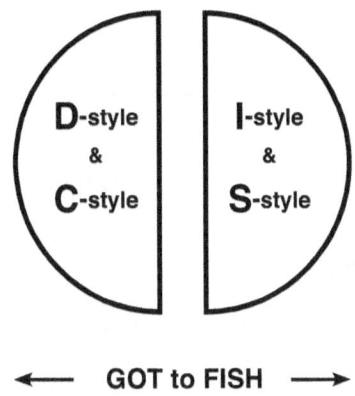

◄—— **GOT to FISH** ——►

Fig. 5.2 Acronym differentiating Task and People

GOT TO FISH

Go with flow or action?
Orientation?
To question/Concerned with?
Teamwork-oriented?
Opens up on feelings more?
Facial Expression and body language?
Intonation—Vocal?
Space—Tactile or not?
How you come to decision?

Play with this and see how you get on. Remember, it won't be something you will pick up straight away as there are many things to remember all in one go. Try it one step at a time, but remember to keep at it You'll be glad you did.

Test, test and test again

Knowing what you now know about the various style types, it is sometimes easy to spot characteristics that you believe belong to one style, and jump to the conclusion that a person is that style. This is not only jumping the gun somewhat, but can also hamper your own learning. Allow yourself to resist the temptation of coming to conclusions too quickly. If you see something, be open to the fact that it is one factor that you have spotted. We are all degrees of one style or another so don't allow one characteristic to cloud your judgement.

Here are things you could do to improve your chances of spotting a style.

Know-nothing state:

When you come from this position, you are not being held to ransom by your own eagerness to get it right straight away, but instead are allowing actions to speak for themselves. Concentrate on the descriptive elements of someone's actions instead of trying to decide what it could mean. This allows you to suspend making a judgement call and merely describe what you see. With enough of these action 'statements', you put yourself in a better place to understand the main style of the other person.

Silence:

Soak in as much information as possible without the temptation to speak too much. Be an observer, master the art of seeing and hearing. In a group situation, focus on the things that are happening around you. When we speak, we miss much of what is happening around us as we become part of the group. Sometimes it is easier to look in from afar as you can pick up more of what is happening around you and how people are interacting.

Multi-dimensional observation:

If you can, take in how someone behaves in numerous situations. So, how are they in a group setting, or in one-to-ones, or on the phone? How do they write their emails? These different settings can help you decipher common traits that may be displayed.

Stressful situations:

What is someone like when the pressure is on? Often, our most 'natural' way of being comes out when we are stressed as we have a tendency to fall back on second-nature habits or go into auto-pilot. During this phase, we are also pushed towards behaving in a certain way by our own need to get out of an uncomfortable place.

Listen out for the language they use:

Do they have a preference for using facts and figures when they are speaking, or do they use more feeling type words that are generic and non-specific? Be careful though, their role could encourage them to use a certain type of language, so then ask yourself how they speak at work when they are more relaxed. Asking open-ended questions during a tea-break could be a way of getting them to relax and express themselves more freely.

Summary

D-style & I-style
(Direct)

D - Open body language
E - 'Telling' style of communication
C - Quick to deal with change
I - Make first move with introductions
D - Make quick decisions
E - Surrounding environment cluttered with paper
R - Take risks in their stride
S - Tend to talk (speech) at a brisk pace

C-style & S-style
(Indirect)

D - Tend to have closed/controlled body language
E - Prefer to 'request' as opposed to 'tell'
C - Cautious or slow in reaction to change
I - Wait for others to make the first move
D - Decision-making can be slow
E - Are quite organised (environment)
R - Tend to be more risk averse
S - Usually speak at a slow/measured pace

D-style & C-style
(Task)

G - Action-focused
O - Task-oriented
T - Concerned with what? Why?
T - Trust mainly their own work
O - Apprehensive at disclosing feelings
F - Restrained expressions, give little away
I - Vocal variety more formal/to the point
S - More protective of personal space
H - Decision-making in a logical/fact-based way

I-style & S-style
(People)

G - Goes with the flow more
O - People-oriented
T - Concerned with who? How?
T - Prefer to work in teams or with others
O - More open about expressing feelings
F - More expressive facial expressions
I - More vocal variety/more informal
S - Can be more tactile
H - Happy to follow their feelings more

Chapter 6

Flexibility and Versatility—
Personal Power

'Knowledge is Power'
Sir Francis Bacon

Knowledge certainly gives you an advantage in most things, but it's what we do with this advantage that makes all the difference. When you have understood what your strengths and behavioural preferences are, it becomes slightly easier to understand someone else's by comparison. When we have knowledge and understanding of others' styles, DISC empowers us to know that their way of behaving is just this, a pattern of behaviour. When we can see it like this, we can apply more perspective to events, which allows us to gain more control of a situation.

One way of gaining control of a situation is through managing our own expectations.

The Expectation Gap

The perceived difference between how we expect someone to behave and how they actually behave gives rise to an expectation gap (see Fig. 6.1). We may not consciously make up our minds about how we expect someone to behave, but a level of expectation is there. For most of us, we expect others to behave not too dissimilar to how we think we behave.

Sabrina is a coach who has been DISC trained. One weekend she invited a friend to stay. They had decided to enjoy a weekend together as they hadn't seen each other for a while. Sabrina wanted to have a relaxing weekend, whereas her friend was more interested in seeing all the sights they agreed to visit and had a list ready. So while Sabrina was fairly relaxed during the weekend in regards to time, her friend was constantly checking her watch to ensure they were on schedule to do all the things they had discussed. This caused a little friction between them and they both went to sleep that first night with this hanging over them. Sabrina, who is an I-style and a secondary S-style realised that the friction was actually caused by their differing styles and expectations. They are friends, but they obviously had their own agendas which had caused this friction. So in the morning, being comfortable with discussing the issue, Sabrina decided to bring what was bothering her out in the open, and to discuss their differing styles and what they both wanted from the weekend. After discussing their expectations, they both appreciated what had been the cause of the previous day's friction, and then having worked on a way forward went back to being comfortable with each other again.

This is a small illustration of how we can learn to discuss differences and expectations, and that by doing so, we can manage our own expectations better while maintaining good relations.

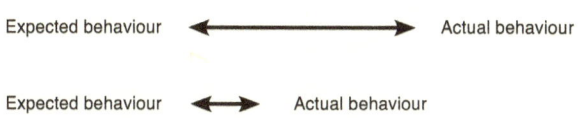

Fig. 6.1 Gap in expectations is reduced with DISC awareness

Through a better understanding of DISC, we can identify a way of behaving which can be distinctly different to the way we normally behave. We may like to think that we can adjust accordingly to someone else's behaviour, especially if it happens to be very different to our own, but when the time comes it is often a different story. No one style finds it easy to adjust to another. We all have to make a conscious shift away from our natural style, which requires effort and perseverance.

Flexibility

> *'If the only tool you have is a hammer, you tend to see*
> *every problem as a nail.'*
> Abraham Maslow

Being able to show flexibility, and 'flexing' to another's behavioural pattern is a way of getting through to the other person in a way that they recognise. It's like speaking their language, their behavioural language. Just like learning to speak another language allows you to communicate easier, understanding someone's pattern and communicating to them in their way allows us to get our message across more effectively.

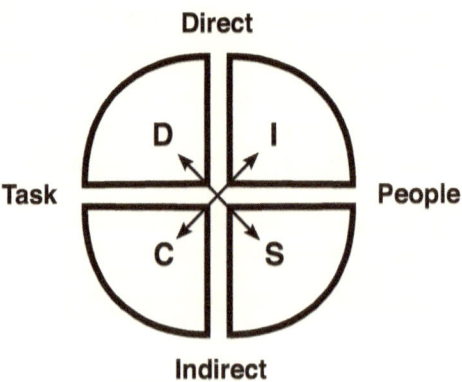

Fig. 6.2 Diagram showing opposite styles

Flexing to the other person's pattern also means you are starting to see things more as the other person is seeing them. The C- and I-styles can be seen as opposites (see Fig. 6.2) as the C-style likes detail, accuracy and facts. The I-style, meanwhile, is not so detail-oriented, shows little patience with items that require high accuracy and prefers working with people than looking at things from a predominantly factual standpoint. So for an I-style, flexing to a C-style would require more diligence in ensuring a piece of work is accurate and looking at the facts before making a decision.

What this effectively means is that, for an I-style, flexing to the C-style is probably as far out as it can get. They are polar opposites in their ways as the I-style is direct and people-focused, and the C-style is indirect and task-focused. So, is it still possible to be both an I-style and a C-style person? You bet it is. Like I mentioned earlier, we all have all four of the DISC elements within us, only the intensity of each element is different, so it isn't unusual to be an I-style in one scenario and then to be more of a C-style in another.

As a manager, being rigid and inflexible doesn't necessarily aid our situation, and neither does it aid our decision-making capabilities. Being able to 'flex' becomes crucial to our performance. As the saying goes, 'you can take a horse to water but you can't make it drink'. Similarly, we can never have total control over another person. What we do have control over is ourselves, and to flex to any situation or person, enables us to retain control of our own mental faculties. Things may not happen, or people may not respond exactly as we would like, but if we can be ready to adapt to the situation we have the option of turning a crisis into an opportunity.

Flexing made easy—your baseline position

One way to flex from one style to another is to look at your starting position, your baseline. What have you got that is closest in common with that style? So if you are a D-style flexing to an I-style, both of you have the directness element in common.

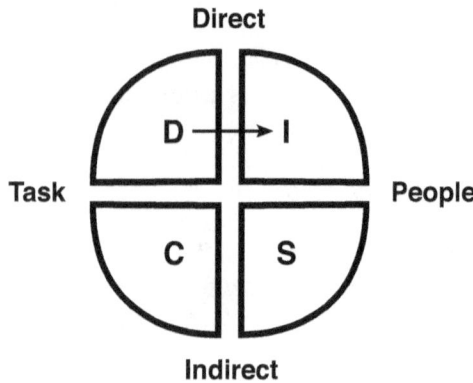

Fig. 6.3 Both D- and I-styles have Direct in common

Being a D-style, knowing that you can keep at your normal brisk pace while communicating with the I-style makes it easier for that communication to flow. At the same time, the D-style needs to flex to the I-style's people-orientation whilst maintaining their strengths too. The D-style can do this by looking at the DECIDERS/GOT-to-FISH template. And because we are going from task-based to people-oriented, we are more concerned with GOT-to-FISH (see previous chapter).

Reframing

Another way to work on your adaptability is through the process of reframing.

Here are some quotes:

1) 'I can't believe he didn't send me the email when he said he was going to.'
2) 'She just bores me with her numbers.'
3) 'He doesn't look like he does much in the office apart from socialise.'
4) 'Why does she have to be so demanding? Who does she think she is?'
5) 'The guy just sits there, never contributing with ideas of his own.'

These are just some quotes that aren't uncommon in the work environment. If we look a little closer we can spot that all of them have styles associated with them. The first quote could be attributed to that of an I-style or D-style. The second is probably a response to the C-style. The third an I-style again. The fourth, a D-style. The final quote could be a response to an S-style. Each of these statements could be valid and yet each statement also comes loaded with an element of judgement. We may not have control of the way the other person has acted, but we certainly have control over the way we decide to see a situation.

And how we see a situation can have a big impact on the way we respond to it. Now read the following statements:

1) 'Maybe it just escaped his mind, so I'll just remind him to send me the email.'
2) 'I think I'll ask her for a summary before we meet.'
3) 'He is obviously doing something right to chat so much and get his work done.'
4) 'At least I know how she can be. I'll remember to keep some room in my work schedule for last minute requests.'
5) 'I'll ask him what he thought of the meeting afterwards to see if he had any other thoughts.'

These statements each 'reframe' the previous statements and are likely to induce another kind of reaction in the person giving them and those listening. The comments are now not loaded with judgement, and enable the focus to be more on what you yourself can do as opposed to merely commenting on the other person.

Reframing a situation can enable us to see a situation in a more positive light, which in turn has less of a dramatic effect on our emotions. It doesn't come naturally for everyone to reframe, especially when we are used to 'shooting from the hip'. But like anything, with practice it can become easier.

Once we become aware of our behaviour, we can then start to have more control over our own actions. And when we are able to control our own actions, we can choose how to behave depending on what the circumstances are, rather than being in a purely reactionary position and at the mercy of the situation we find ourselves in.

Our Toolbox

We have seen it time and again in the workplace; we use the same management tactics with all our staff and yet some of our team members react more positively than others. For those that don't respond how we would like, we attribute it to some reason or another, and yet we persist with the same method. Thinking and working in this way will not help the situation. Our frustrations will begin to affect the way we treat different members of the team whether we like it or not. Take, for example, an idea that has just come to you. You get excited and share it with someone in the hope that they can also see what a wonderful idea it is. However, somehow they don't share the same level of enthusiasm. You pretend not to listen to their view, but in time it slowly affects how you see the idea. You don't realise it at the time but before the idea has gone any further, it has died an early death. It's why many people have ideas, but they just don't get past the first hurdle—momentum is lost.

When someone hasn't responded to your management/personal style, you can go one of two ways. You can either hope that they eventually do respond (which is out of your control), or try another method. If this doesn't work how many of us are willing to try another way?

On a training day, there were eight colleagues in a rowing boat. Two in the middle were rowing and three were sitting at either end of the boat. The rowers tried to row in sync with each other but as soon as they began, one rower would row faster than the other and instead of going forwards (or backwards, as is the case in rowing), they went round in a circle. They thought they'd try again, using the same tactic, as maybe they weren't starting off properly. Again, the same result. So they decided to change tactics. One would call out some signals so that both rowers would respond to this command. It worked better but they still found themselves going round as one of the rowers was responding

---

and the other rower was going at his own pace. They changed tactics once more and this time one caller opposite each of the rowers called out so each rower would just focus on the person ahead of them. Again, while this was successful to a degree, having more than one person navigating added an extra element of confusion to the process. So they thought of altering the message once more. They reverted back to one person shouting out aloud, with that same person also imitating a rowing motion. This worked a treat for the rowers and they both began to work in sync. The rowers got excited about the fact they were going straight and they weren't even trying so hard.

Through trial and error this group were able to get feedback as to what was working and what was not. They were better able to respond as a team to the visual as well as verbal cue.

Plan, Do, Check, ACT!

With the DISC system, we are able to ask ourselves the question: how can I adapt what I am saying/doing so that it gets through to the other person effectively? By doing this, we are taking personal responsibility for the message being communicated instead of relying on the recipient to just 'get it'.

William Edwards Deming[7] is best known for being one of the pioneers of the Japanese management technique known as Quality Management, and who came up with the Plan-Do-Check-Act (PDCA) cycle, also known as the Deming Cycle (see Fig. 6.4). PDCA was invented as a way of continually testing a process until it becomes right. Similarly, this approach can also be used when trying to understand which behaviours enable us to adapt to the person we are with.

---

[7]   Obtained online from the Balanced Scorecard Institute 1998: http://www.balancedscorecard. org/thedemingcycle/tabid/112/default.aspx

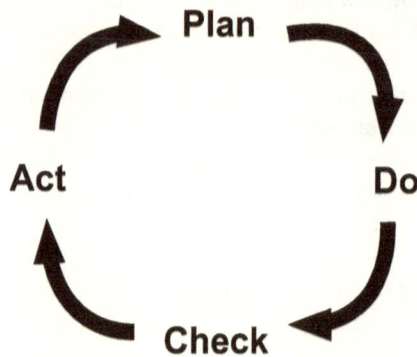

Fig. 6.4 The Plan-Do-Check-Act cycle

Plan

Understand where your preferred behaviour style lies and where you think the style of the other person lies. You then have to ascertain which behaviours you want to adjust to, and how you are going to achieve this. To do this effectively, it's useful to have a target to aim for. For example, here are two results you may want to achieve from an interaction.

1. You want to get the person to see the benefits of budgeting. However, they are more people-oriented and have previously not shown much interest when you start talking numbers. In fact they switch off at the mere mention of figures.
2. You want to come out of the meeting with action points agreed, something that has eluded you many times in the past.

These are tangible outcomes for which temporary flexing is necessary, and where you can get instant feedback as a result of your actions.

Do

Take action and consciously adjust your behaviour to match that of the recipient, maintaining rapport at all times (GOT-to-FISH?).

Be mindful of specific differences in style between your behaviour and theirs. Go prepared and visualise beforehand how they are, so that you are prepared for their specific ways. Make a mental note of these ways so that you have them signposted at specific junctures in your interaction.

Check

This is feedback. What is their actual response to the target (1) or (2) in comparison to how you expected their response to be? Calibrating this can give you an indication of how you are doing and what to do next time.

Act!

Based on the 'check' you can ascertain whether you adapted sufficiently and how you can improve for next time. The more you are able to look at your own behaviour and put yourself in the other person's shoes, the more you can appreciate their position and put it into a wider context.

This is where much of your learning happens, as you are able to understand what works and what doesn't. The more practice you get at being adaptable, the more resourceful you can become and the better the connection you can have with others.

Once you have evaluated, go through the cycle once again and keep improving your skills.

One of the challenges of adaptability is knowing when to adapt, and when not to. You can't go through life adapting to absolutely everything. You'll be a nervous wreck before you know it, and will no doubt lose yourself in the process. Being adaptable means adjusting to the circumstances (be it a person or situation) in the attainment of our goals because this is what governs our actions—our goals. When we can see our goal as clearly as summer daylight, adapting to make it happen takes on a whole new meaning and stretches our mind to a whole new level.

Increasing your versatility

> *'A man's mind once stretched may never return to its*
> *original dimensions again'*
> George Bernard Shaw

As discussed already, we all have each of the four styles within us. Yes, we have our strengths, and this is the place we most like to and want to be. However, it isn't always feasible for us to stay in this place and what is required is to tap into the 'other' you. Different situations require different responses. And to use de Bono speak, when we need to be more versatile, we need to put on a different hat[8]. It's a bit like an off-road vehicle: on the road we have it on one type of setting, but on more rough terrain we need to make the switch to a setting that is going to respond better to the new surface. And indeed, it is useful to have the option in your car to be able to do this.

How can you switch from one mode to another? Is it really that easy?

If you are an S-style and find it difficult to carry out a specific element of your job (which requires making quick-fire decisions), how can you improve in this area?

Like everything, it requires application and practise. And the more you practise, the better you will become at tapping into the other you. I use this term because, as mentioned, we all have elements of each of the four styles in us, only some are more dominant than others.

One way to understand how you can tap into the other you is to go into your memory bank and pull out some previous experiences. We all have some experiences related to each of the four different styles. Obviously, for our preferred style, we'll have plenty of examples. So think of the strengths for each of the other styles and then consider a situation or time when you have exhibited this strength in the past. For instance, the C-style is good at:

- Work that requires attention to detail
- Completing what they have started

---

[8]   de Bono, E. (1985), *Six Thinking Hats* (Little, Brown and Company)

- Being analytical
- Looking for ways of improving current processes.

At a training company, Tom is a sales manager, a dominant I- and D-style, respectively, and who wants to communicate to Mike, the academic manager and C-style dominant, that he has ideas on how Mike can improve the company's academic programme. Tom has spoken with some students and the feedback he's getting is that the students aren't being engaged with some of the sessions—class attendance is at an average of 60%, although pass rates are steady at 70%. There is much scope for improvement, however, so Tom has decided that the best place to discuss this is at their weekly one-to-one. These meetings often have a loose agenda and it's generally a catch-up between the two managers on how their respective departments are performing.

Due to the sensitive nature of this one topic that directly affects the academic department, Tom decides that it is better to place it as an agenda item and for Mike to be aware beforehand so that he can come pre-prepared, at least mentally.

So looking at the PDCA cycle:

Plan—Tom to speak with Mike about areas of the programme that could be improved.

Do—Tom mentions the issue at one of his weekly meetings with Mike. The main point is that the students have tended to see the classes as just another class, when there is scope for making the classes more interesting. Feedback forms tend to be handed out at the end of the term and they haven't been too teaching-centric, rather the focus has been on the facilities of the training centre etc.

Check—During the meeting, Tom realises that Mike is getting defensive because the feedback forms have been showing that students are relatively satisfied with the teaching, and a pass mark of 70% has been consistent for much of the year (the course has only been running for a year).

ACT!—After the meeting, Tom analyses how the meeting went and how close he came to achieving the goal. In this instance, Mike didn't take into consideration much of what Tom had mentioned and the meeting was adjourned without any real resolution.

So Tom decided to take another route.

Plan—To speak with Mike about the core areas of the programme and whether the feedback form can have a variety of questions assessing the quality of the teaching.

Do—Spoke with Mike about improving the feedback form, which resulted in the Sales team re-writing the form with the input of the Education team.

Check—Over the coming weeks feedback was gathered from the students and analysed. It was discovered that attendance was down as students felt they didn't get much from the class, and that revision near the end of the course helped them catch up on items missed.

ACT!—So the Education team went about re-drafting some of the course content which they hoped would add more value for the students, and they also mixed the programme up a bit. The combined impact was that the course became less predictable which increased students' interest. This especially benefitted those students for whom school wasn't necessarily a great experience.

As a result, average class attendance increased to 80% and the overall pass rate increased to 84%.

If it was up to Tom, he would have made an immediate change to the programme as soon as he had spoken with the students. However, he was savvy enough to understand that Mike (a C-style) needed more than just a hunch and word-of-mouth feedback from a few students to be convinced. So Tom went about working with Mike to carry out more research and let the results speak for themselves. It took more time, and stretched Tom's patience who likes to do things a lot quicker, but it had the effect of bringing the Education team on board and maintaining relations between the two departments.

Summary

We have all developed our own styles over time and no one style is more adaptable than another. It just comes down to whether you as an individual want to adapt or not.

Remember, adapting is something that we do as a temporary measure. It is not a long-term thing, so we aren't looking at it being something permanent.

The PDCA cycle is a simple way of consistently trying to do this.

Plan
What is your style? What is the other person's? How can you adjust what you do to get through to the other person more effectively?

Do
Take action.

Check
Calibrate their response.

ACT!
Ascertain whether what you did to adapt helped you to glean the response that you required. If not, then revisit the planning stage, and try out something else. Persevere and try out different things, in line with what the other person's style is.

Chapter 7

Management Uses

Strategies for Management

In the fast-moving world that we occupy, where information is required quicker and more accurately than ever before, never has so much been demanded from the managers of today. Information can reach the furthest places in a matter of seconds and if this information isn't accurate, then the fallout can be quite severe.

Managers, therefore, need to demonstrate they have full control of their departments and at the same time, with their ever-expanding workload, ensure work is appropriately spread amongst the team so that resources are used effectively.

One of the biggest modern day fallacies has been the notion that technology will make our lives easier. If anything, it seems to have gone the other way. We are being bombarded with more information than ever before, we are required to respond faster than ever before, and our workload—rather than decreasing—has actually increased. Our workplaces have dwindling staff numbers with the work being shared out amongst the remaining staff. And regardless of how much work a manager has to do, team members still want to be valued and treated with respect. One of the biggest challenges facing managers today is keeping hold of their best staff. Bad relations with a direct line manager and lack of growth in a role are two common reasons for employees leaving their jobs. Losing good staff costs organisations money and time in recruitment and from new employees getting up to speed with the job. This can also have a knock-on effect on the rest of the team.

Treating each member of your direct team in a manner they want to be treated can go a long way in ensuring you retain your best staff. The Chartered Institute of Personnel and Development (CIPD) in the UK says that people are more likely to stay in a job that they like and in one that they feel they can grow, over another job that is going to simply pay more.

At school one of my best teachers was Mr McDonald. We can all remember a best teacher from our schooldays—the teacher who managed to get the best out of us and who we would go that extra mile for; the teacher who we could connect with and who we felt could make us work to our potential. Well, it can happen in organisations too. Sports operate no differently to organisations. Just like in organisations where teamplay is important, man-management skills are crucial.

Sports coaches who have distinguished themselves have been ones who, like our favourite teachers, have been able to manage the individual players as well as improving the team as a whole.

In the world of soccer, Carlo Ancelotti is one such manager who was described as such by David Beckham[9] who played under him at AC Milan:

'Carlo Ancelotti's man-management skills are exceptional. He is a brilliant coach.

'To have played under a manager of his quality is a real privilege. He is one of the greats. I have been lucky in my career to play under a few of the best in the business and he comes into that category. I just wish I had been able to play for him for many more years. It has been a lot of fun.

'Every single one of the Milan players adores him and doesn't want him to go. They are pleading with him to stay. I know wherever he goes, and whatever he does, he will always have my admiration and respect.'

No doubt Carlo Ancelotti knows how to manage each individual member of his team. Here, we are going to be looking at each of the styles and the possible ways in which each of them can be nurtured and developed.

---

[9] David Beckham quote, taken from *The Guardian*: http://www.guardian.co.uk/football/2009/may/19/beckham-ancelotti-chelsea-milan

Managing the D-style

'If you can't take the heat, then get out of the kitchen'
Sen. H. S. Truman

'It's my way, or the highway.'
Anonymous

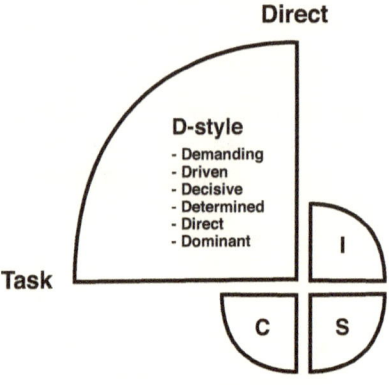

Fig. 7.1 Traits of the D-style

Stephen, a manager, was very task-focused and not that people-oriented. When colleagues saw him walking down the corridor, they would get out of his way thinking he was in an angry mood, when he was actually deep in thought about something and his walk was just how he walked when he was thinking 'on the move'. Unfortunately for Stephen, most of his colleagues were either I- or S-styles who misconstrued his behaviour as unfriendly. So although the quality of his work was great, Stephen didn't get on so well with his peers who judged him to come across as arrogant and rather aloof. After speaking with him, it became clear that the only thing really on his mind most of the time was work and that people were mistaking his outward actions as meaning something else. For the purposes of good team spirit, it was felt this was a good area for him to look at.

So because Stephen was naturally more task-focused, I looked at ways in which he could use this to come across better to others within the company. Due to his acute task-oriented focus, we made relating with others a task. Because he used his calendar for everything, he put into his calendar times of the day when he would go out and mingle with others in the organisation. This reframing of connecting with others as a task, made all the difference to Stephen and his department. Over time, people started to perceive him differently as he now approached them more and talked not only about work. They also saw him as being more approachable and came to understand him more after seeing more of him.

The D-style is very much bottom-line, task-focused. This person likes their space and whether you like it or not, they want to have control.

Just like their motto, whether they are leading or following, in their eyes they are always the leader. They like to have things go their way so allow them the space to make their own decisions. Micro-management doesn't work for a D-style person. Quick thinkers who like to see the big picture, D-style people are always going to be pushing the boundaries. The only boundaries they like adhering to are their own. Even then, they aren't averse to over-riding what they themselves put into place.

To get through to the D-style, they need to know you aren't a pushover and have researched sufficiently. This is a highly assertive type and unless you stay firm but fair, this type will like to assert their way above authority, which they tend to see as a hindrance. The D-style tends to perform better in an environment that is focused on the bottom-line and is fast-moving. A results-focused, competitive environment is the kind of environment a D-style would thrive in.

Due to their penchant for control of their surroundings, you are more likely to get the most out of the D-style if you just let them get on with it. However, give them full rein at your peril, so agree freedom of action within certain parameters and what the end result should be. Telling the D-style what to do doesn't go down well with this type so allow them the freedom of figuring out how to get there, once you've communicated to them what the end result should be.

If you need to show them what you are looking for, give them the big picture first and then 'chunk down'. Chunking down is an NLP (Neuro Linguistic Programming) term meaning to break down into smaller segments. So although the D-style doesn't really want to know the details if they don't need to have them, they may want to know the basics of how something functions, or at least where the baseline is. Once they work out the gist of how something operates, allow them to work out the rest for themselves. Because of their penchant for action and getting things done, they will play with it and try to find a better or quicker way of doing something.

Being big on status, if you do have to correct them on something do it behind closed doors. Competition of any sort is a pastime of theirs and with their competitive spirit, they tend not to like losing. Maybe it's because they aren't used to it. The D-style is resilient and although they don't like to be told they can improve (unless they see it for themselves) it needs to be said in a direct way supported with facts.

They tend to take criticism badly and can be sore losers, but they will want to prove themselves if the other person can demonstrate that they have a point.

'Kevin, it has consistently been the case that when you are late in the office, the others are stretched and we miss sales calls in the morning as a result. This costs us over £X each time and over the course of the year can cost us up to £X in lost sales. Please can you reflect on how we are going to make up for this and how you can make it into work on time from now on?'

As they are bottom-line focused, let them know the result you are looking for, and by when, and then allow them to figure out how to get there.

The key to managing the D-style is setting parameters and then allowing them to get on with it.

Motivation and the D-style

We all get motivated by different things. For some a day out with the team is a brilliant way of getting to know each other better. For others, this is a nightmare scenario and they'd much rather stay behind their desks and get on with their work. As a manager it is important to get to know your individual team members and what drives them, as you then have more of a profile on each and can manage them accordingly.

D-styles are motivated by power and authority. In a team setting, if they aren't the leader by role, then they will assume a leader role through sheer personality. So one way you can keep them motivated is to empower them to make their own decisions within the scope of their role. This freedom will allow them to thrive in their drive for results.

When communicating with the D-style, they tend not to be interested in small talk so be sure to communicate to the point and give them the big picture. With their focus on efficiency, the D-style prefers to know what it is that needs to be achieved. In their own way, their preference is to focus on the solution to the problem. Being solvers of problems is what they are particularly good at so once you are sure they know what is expected of them, leave them to get on with it.

When they have to decide on something, they tend to be keen on getting the bottom-line facts and then making a decision. Giving them masses of details with no structure is likely to turn them off; especially if it's not immediately obvious what the problem is (patience isn't necessarily a D-style's strong point). So be prepared in a structured way, be certain you know what you are asking for (especially if you are an S-style) and as succinctly as possible, ask away.

This style likes the stimulation a challenge brings, but their efforts must show results. When they see something that they don't like, the D-style will see that it gets changed. And they will want others to help them achieve it too. They may not possess the seamless influential techniques of the I-style but they will find a way of doing what they want anyway—even if this means doing it themselves and cutting a few corners. In the D-style, you have someone who wants their effort to be valued.

When speaking with them, try focusing on the 'what'. Keep the 'how' to a minimum as they could easily just switch off. Speak their language (firm and direct), and they will respond accordingly.

Feedback and Praise

Being task-oriented, they like to be recognised for their achievements. Despite their sometimes brash exterior, if you catch the D-style at the right moment, they will welcome your comments. When commending them, let them know what it is for. Feint praise doesn't work for this type as 'they know they are good anyway. It's just taken you this long to realise it!'

Catch them in full-flow and you'll think they have just brushed your feedback aside and aren't interested, when they may just be focused on the task currently at hand. When you are giving feedback ensure that they aren't preoccupied with something—a weekly meeting of some sort or an appraisal meeting is a more appropriate time to give praise for good work done. You are more likely to catch them in listening mode. You will also find them more in a listening mood when they are feeling good about something. Take the opportunity, and ask them for a moment.

D-styles tend to respond better when feedback is delivered in a firm, direct and task-oriented fashion. Better to mention how:

'I appreciated the way that you…' or that
'I noticed when you… great work!'

The D-style prefers praise in this deliberate way than just getting praise for praise's sake. They pride themselves on their work and their achievements above anything else.

Like all communication to the D-style, keep it brief and move on. This style likes action and doing things and when they have done something, they briskly move onto the next item.

With the D-style's tendency to need control, allow them to make up for their weaknesses. Highlight to them where exactly you believe they can improve and then allow them to think about how this can be done. If nothing is immediately forthcoming, try not to spend too much time going over it. Agree with them a timeframe to come back to you. This enables the D-style to retain control and at the same time allows you to get them to focus on what actions they need to take to improve certain areas.

Delegating to the D-style

The D-style likes to show a 'know-it-all' attitude. Big-picture-oriented, when delegating a piece of work to them, approach it so that you bring them into the picture immediately. Their mind will already have moved two big steps in that direction. With their pragmatic outlook, the D-style is likely to want to do something if they see the need to do it. So don't expect them to accept the work you hand over without them questioning it. If they do question, it isn't necessarily because they want to be awkward, although they are never shy of confrontation, but more out of a willingness to understand the need for it.

Stand firm and be prepared. They think very quickly on their feet so the more prepared you are the better your outcome is likely to be of getting them to come on board.

Decision-making and the D-style

D-styles are not shy when it comes to decision-making. To ensure they are not going to run away with making all the decisions, try setting the ground rules early on. Ensure they know what they can decide on and what they can't. Show them what area is theirs to look at so that they are aware of the parameters. By bringing them in to see the bigger picture, you allow them room to 'breathe' and make more informed decisions. Micro-managing this style will stifle them and be counter-productive. So giving smaller projects to them to manage, depending on their skillset, is something that would work for them.

D-styles are quick decision makers and are eager to get on with things. Sometimes, in their haste to get things moving along, they may decide to do something a little too quickly, without due care and attention. Get them to slow down and to show you in logical steps how they came up with their decision. This may also help them to see what you are looking for and encourage them to think it through properly first before running it by you.

They don't usually lack confidence and are not afraid to take risks, so tug on their responsibility strings and make them aware of how it affects others and, ultimately, themselves. They want to be seen to be doing the right thing, especially if it affects their promotional chances in some way.

Problem solving skills of the D-style

D-styles are natural problem solvers, so allow them space to come up with solutions for themselves. Ask them what they think. When they do come up with solutions, allow them to see for themselves the results. D-styles prefer to work on their own and on their own terms so allow them this space and time to try out their ideas. The agreeing of parameters, as mentioned earlier, gives them a guide of what they can do on their own initiative and what they need to run by you first. So if their idea works, they'll feel more confident going forward and if it doesn't work, they wouldn't feel too pressured as you'd have endorsed their idea at the outset anyway.

However, this doesn't mean you allow them to have it all their own way. As mentioned earlier, they don't mind getting feedback so long as it makes sense to them. Being combative, they may even put up a stance and tell you what they think, so challenge them by focusing on the task and allow them to see the problem in a wider context.

Sometimes, what they say may not come off, but they are quick learners; allow them to figure out what went wrong and to feed this back to you.

Responding to change

The D-style thrives in times of change, as they are usually the ones at the forefront of it all. However, taking in the strategic view, they have the bigger picture in mind and prefer to be engaged with the change process, regardless of their position in the hierarchical structure. In an episode of Gordon Ramsay's *Kitchen*

Nightmares[10], a restaurant was in need of a complete turnaround (which is the general objective of the show). Gordon spoke with the people involved with the restaurant and one particular waiter was forthright in his view of 'sack the owner, only then will things change!'

Whether the waiter was right or not, I can't imagine an S-style or C-style being so forthcoming with their views, even if it was a valid one. With the C-style, even if they did want this, they'd come out with logical reasons why this could be the preferred course of action and would not articulate it directly as this waiter did.

The D-style people really are the change agents!

Things to watch out for

As managers, these are some areas we should consider in regards to our team members to be able to manage them proactively.

The D-style does tend to take on more than they can chew. Do ensure they are doing fine with what they are currently working on. They aren't going to mention that they are struggling as, to them, this could suggest a sign of weakness so as a result of their drive to win, they like to think they can handle anything that comes their way. Signs that they could be taking on too much are irritability and more-than-usual aggressive behaviour with their colleagues. A good holiday is maybe just what's needed.

One way to ensure they are on top of their targets is to monitor their progress at certain agreed intervals. This way, they don't feel crammed by your management style and you also get to see how they are progressing with their tasks.

Being a style of action, sometimes it could be inaction that is the best form of action. D-styles are not known for their patience. If things aren't going their way, or are not going as well as they had hoped, then their tendency to control the situation takes over. This is another reason for them to be prone to aggression and

---

[10] *Kitchen Nightmares USA*, A. Smith & Co productions

more direct behaviour. Gone too far, this can put undue strain on relationships which can affect overall team morale.

Managing the I-style

'Work hard, play harder'
Anonymous

'All work and no play makes Jack a dull boy'
Anonymous

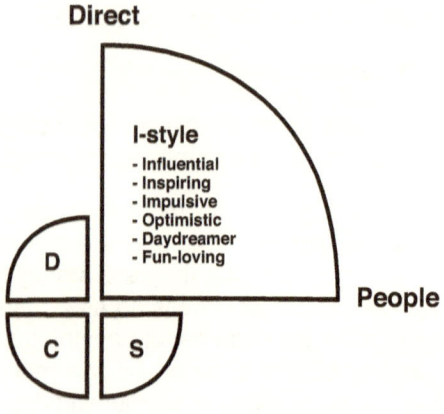

Fig. 7.2 Traits of the I-style

The I-style is someone who enjoys the people side of business. They like coming into work to engage with their fellow colleagues. Regardless of where in the hierarchical structure people operate, the I-style tends to mix well with them. They have usually made friends in whatever activity they are involved in so are generally well-connected in the organisation.

Like the D-style, the I-style likes to have a certain amount of freedom in which to operate. Whilst they prefer working with others than on their own, they like to be afforded a certain amount of space to operate and to 'spread their wings'. Creativity is their thing so activities that allow them to dream up ideas and work with others will really appeal to the I-style type. And because they like to think 'outside-the-box', they are usually bustling with new ideas.

Although I-styles will be full of ideas and work out ways to implement them, they may have a tendency to not always follow through on their initial enthusiasm. One way to manage this would be to schedule meetings in advance so you can get together to measure progress. You could maybe ask them to put in place a plan of what they will do and by when, so that it can be followed and you can monitor it. This would allow the I-style to work at their own pace and allow you to monitor their progress.

Motivation and the I-style

Because their motivation is largely extrinsic, give them roles where they can be identified clearly for their contributions. Show them appreciation for their efforts as they'll respond to this and give you tons of effort in return. Connect with them by allowing them time to share information about themselves. Once you show genuine interest in them, they want to share information about their likes and dislikes so spend some time getting to know them, it'll help set the foundation for better relations in the future. Not everyone is inclined this way, the D-style being one of them. The D-style isn't into small talk and building connections with others unless they see a clear reason for doing so. With the I-style, however, they like to have the peace of mind to know you get along.

Although everyone in some way, shape or form likes to be recognised for their achievements, recognition acts as an additional motivator for this type more than it does for the other styles. When I-styles are proud of their achievements they want to share this with others, no matter who they are. So being people-oriented, a mention during a group meeting of what they are up to would really help them feel like they are contributing.

The I-style likes the freedom of space to think. They welcome being given free-rein to come up with ideas for improvement, making more money, better marketing strategies, whatever. So being a natural dreamer, this type loves to spend time on 'blue-sky thinking'. They are the creative beings of the four main styles and can inspire just as easily as be inspired.

Ian is an accountant who prefers to work with others in finding solutions to their problems, rather than sit in front of his computer building models on spreadsheets. Even with his heavy workload, where he spends his time working late into the evenings (often leaving the office at 10 p.m.), he jumped at the opportunity of contributing to the company newsletter on a monthly basis. It was an opportunity for him to showcase himself and his ideas to the rest of the organisation. Sue, his manager, was conscious of the excessive amount of time he often spent in the office, which she knew he could reduce through more effective working, so she made it a development point for him to figure out a way to reduce the hours he spent in the office if he wanted to take on the additional work of the newsletter. With the lure of the newsletter, through looking at his planning and prioritising the way he works, Ian soon found better ways of working and spending more time working on the things he likes.

As mentioned earlier, to the I-style, what others say about them matters. So if they know that their name is going to be attached to a piece of work, they'll want to give it their best shot.

Feedback and Praising the I-style

When feeding back to the I-style, keep it upbeat and positive. For instance, if you wanted to discuss some areas of improvement, take a similar approach to when feeding back something positive. Something like:

'You are a much valued member of the team and one area you may need to look at is your time-keeping, as it has affected others in the office on a few occasions. And because you are a valued member, if you're not there when the meeting kicks off your fellow team members sometimes get the impression that you don't value their time, when I think this isn't the message you want to get across at all. Do you have any ideas on how you can improve your time-keeping and how you can monitor this?'

The combination of the people side of things, with an emphasis on follow-through will tend to have more of an impact on the I-style than just general feedback, as this will help focus their mind on a strategy and tangible targets. Also think about allowing time for them to give you feedback in return for what you have said. They like to have their say and allowing them this time (and directly encouraging them to express what they are thinking) can demonstrate to them you are willing to listen and consider what they have to say.

When they are in their creative 'zone', be mindful of the I-style's contribution. If an idea doesn't seem quite right or seems a bit far-fetched, ask them to build on it in a certain direction rather than discounting it outright. They are more likely to respond to an encouraging tone than one they perceive as being non-appreciative of their efforts.

When praising the I-style, try something like 'when you were out there promoting the charity to the local community, we had plenty of interest because of your passion coming through—this was common feedback we got from many people who attended the open day'. It puts them in the picture and really drives home how they made an impact on others.

As for timing, any time is a good time to praise an I-style. With their need for external recognition, praise is something that invigorates them and makes them feel good about themselves. So you can choose to compliment them one-to-one or in a group setting, they are comfortable with both.

Delegating to the I-style

When delegating to the I-style, show them the bigger picture and try not to micro-manage. So help them see the bottom-line and what you want to achieve. Give them signposts of what you expect and when.

These signposts should be agreed with them and put down in writing, maybe on a follow-up email. Because of their likelihood of getting distracted, help them stay focused by giving them targets and deadlines. Following this up with quick meetings will help you discover early on whether they are on the right track or not, without them feeling too constrained.

Sometimes, knowing what not to delegate is just as important as delegating. If you have a piece of work that requires repetition and accuracy, then the I-style is probably not the type to do it. You may find that the amount of time you saved in delegating the work has now been wasted on spotting their errors. Consistency and accuracy are not strong points of the I-style. Whether this is because they get bored easily, or cannot maintain concentration for certain periods of time, is unique to the individual. What is apparent is they like to do things their own way, and their way (they can be quite stubborn about this) isn't always the best way for producing accurate work.

Managing their growth areas

Similar to the D-style, as they are likely to be involved with many things, getting them to keep a written schedule can have a massive impact on keeping them on track. Being confident in their own ability, they may speak a good game, but follow through is not always as it could be.

One way of getting them to complete their objectives, is to help them become more structured. They usually aren't great with detail so showing them quick-fire techniques of cutting out simple errors can get them into the habit of adopting best practice. They may not want to focus on this element of their work, but when they see the results for themselves and how it can save them time and stress, you'll find it easier to get them on board with your way of thinking.

While he was dedicated to his work, Ian had a less-than-systematic way of keeping on top of his paperwork. He was great on the phone getting new clients through cold-calling, but often didn't follow up with them and didn't keep notes of conversations he'd had with clients in the past. Due to the sheer volume of calls that he made, apart from the odd memorable conversations, it was difficult to keep track of people and what they had specifically spoken about on previous occasions. His manager Dave noted that Ian was losing time looking for bits of information that were in various places, which added to Ian's level of stress. So Dave scheduled in time to go through with Ian a way of keeping a simple system that he could use going forward. The simplicity of the system enabled Ian to see the benefit of having a process that kept his information in one place and which was easy to access whenever he wanted. More importantly, it made sure Ian had more time to do the things he liked instead of worrying about the things he didn't, like the administrative side of his work.

Responding to change

The I-style embraces change as it's an opportunity for them to try something new. I-styles like to explore new things, even at the expense of what they are currently doing which can then be left incomplete. It's perhaps unsurprising that the S-style and C-style are weary of this 'non-completion' trait of the I-style as it means they can't rely on them to complete what they say they are going to.

This type, being the social butterfly that they are, may also see change as an opportunity to work with a new team, and meet new people. Their ability to engage directly with their surroundings means they are able to adapt more easily to a change in circumstances.

It is good to know that during a change programme, there is a type of person that can fill the rest of the team with hope at uncertain times and that change is not necessarily a bad thing. That it can be a time for exploring new things, which can also be a positive.

Not everyone will share their enthusiasm but at least you'll have a champion for change by your side.

Managing the S-style

'Better to be safe than sorry'
Anonymous

A bird in hand is worth two in the bush
English Proverb

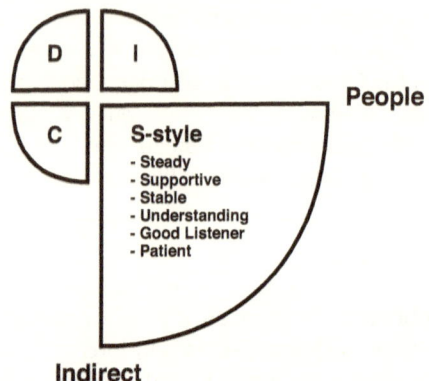

Fig. 7.3 Traits of the S-style

The S-style is the person you can depend on. Show appreciation for their efforts and they'll take two steps towards you. Not really a style that displays too many histrionics, they would much rather work at a steady pace and get the work done methodically. If there is a type that likes their daily routine at work, the S-style is it. They may come in, have a quick chat whilst making themselves a cup of tea and preparing their desk for the day ahead. They get comfort in the knowledge that they know what they are going to be doing for the rest of the day. Give them the work and they will just get on with the task at hand.

Be Patient

Be patient with them. This style prefers you show them how you want something to be done, step-by-step, and they'll take good notes. The natural tendency for the D- and I-style manager is to hurry their S-style colleague, for them to catch on quickly. However, unless they know what they are doing, this won't get the best out of them. So the main thing when working with the person who employs the S-style behaviour is to slow down a little and give clear instructions; allow them time to absorb the information. It may not always be feasible to allow someone to work at their own pace, especially if deadlines are looming. However, the S-style is likely to get going when they know exactly what they are doing, and how they are going to do it. So if you need to spend time with your team members individually, spend it with the S-style members first. They may need more of your initial time for a briefing before they get going. If you find yourself short on time, which is common these days, mention it to the S-style before you start. This way, they are aware and can prime themselves to go a little faster. Do reassure them that if they don't quite follow 100% right now, that's fine and you can always go through the points they aren't clear on a little later.

When you take the S-style through a step-by-step process it enables them to see how all the sequences fit logically together and how an activity is done. They don't necessarily want to re-invent the wheel (leave that to the other styles) and will do it exactly how you show them.

The S-style is not the type to draw attention to themselves, and are more eager just to be able to get on with the task at hand. Not being attention-seekers they prefer to see themselves as team players. They do like to be recognised for the work that they do so acknowledge their efforts.

The one thing that the S-style wants to have is security: the security of knowing what is going to happen next, and what to prepare for. Unless it is for birthdays, engagements etc, they don't generally like surprises at work. So try creating an environment that is friendly and supportive, a place where they can feel 'safe'.

This involves a workplace where there is group cooperation as they enjoy being part of and working as a team. Their ideal role is that of a supportive lieutenant, although they can also make effective leaders.

Sue was an integral part of the team who knew her role well. As she got on top of what she was doing, she was more than happy to help out one of her colleagues Ellen—an I-style—who was struggling to meet a few deadlines (no surprises there!). So Sue's manager Phil explained the role to Sue, who was expecting to help Ellen type out a few letters and do other admin work, nothing too strenuous. In the event, however, Ellen passed along work with vague instructions of what to do. It was obvious there was more to it than Sue's manager had made out. But not wanting to let down either Phil or Ellen, Sue went about giving it her best shot. When Phil asked Sue how it was going she said fine. It wasn't though. The work started to take up more of her time with the strain beginning to show and she started missing her own deadlines.

This situation could have been averted if Phil had asked Ellen to show him the work that she wanted Sue to do. He then could have been clearer with Sue as to the actual work involved, and sat in initially with Ellen and Sue for the handover of the work. This would have provided more clarity around the type of work Sue was having handed to her. They may then have decided earlier on that the work wasn't suitable to hand over to Sue in its current form. As it happens, these checks weren't made which meant Sue got caught up in doing some work she was never quite prepared for.

Motivation and the S-style

What tends to motivate the S-style is knowing what they are doing. They take comfort with the status quo and with maintaining it. They would much rather stick to a tried and trusted method that seems to work than replace it with something that is unknown and potentially risky, even if the benefits are obvious.

In the workplace, one way they get themselves comfortable is by creating a warm aura around their desks with pictures of loved ones. They tend to be family-oriented and their family or friends can form the focal point of their lives. Be understanding of this as they may value flexibility of time with their family over financial rewards. Obviously each of our personal situations dictate what we want out of work, but having a supportive manager who is flexible in identifying individual needs can play a big part in keeping staff motivated. S-styles like to know that they are doing a good job, so as much as is possible, try to keep this style abreast of how you think they are doing and keep them informed of any major changes.

Show them, through rewards if possible, that they aren't being taken for granted and that if they continue to provide good consistent service, they will be recognised for it. To this effect, give them tangible targets to aim for which they can measure themselves against.

In a team, they tend to be motivated most when they know their role and how it fits in with the rest of the team. For example, during a pitstop in a Formula 1 race, the team are well versed on their individual roles. Although it is a high-pressured scenario, the S-style is still able to perform perfectly well under pressure as they know exactly what it is required of them and what they need to focus on. They also have the comfort of knowing that the training they have received has prepared them for it.

Equally, what is likely to demotivate an S-style are constant interruptions. They have completer-finisher tendencies and like to get on with it. As they are more of a passive behavioural type, assertiveness is not one of their strengths, so they are just likely to accept interruptions to their work, even if they don't like it. They won't show their displeasure until it is too late (when they may behave out of character), so if you're not sure how they feel, ask them.

Knowing that they are good at their role is motivation in itself for the S-style. And they only know this if you inform them of it so don't hold back in commending good work.

Feedback and praising the S-style

As the saying goes, feedback is the breakfast of champions, and if they aren't doing a good enough job, they want to know why and be shown how it should actually be done. With the S-style, time is what they require from you. Once they have this and are comfortable with how to do something, you can then leave them to get on with it. With regards to the timing of giving feedback, as long as they have an idea that you are going to give them feedback, any time is a reasonable time to speak with them. Highlight clearly where they have performed well and where you feel they could improve further. When feeding back keep it light, do it in a reassuring manner and for areas of improvement, comment specifically on the activity itself rather than them as a person.

Not normally one who is comfortable with the spotlight, unlike the I-style, they prefer acknowledgement for teamwork and their role within it. Give individual praise in a one-to-one setting. This way they can digest it better without feeling self-conscious and worrying about what others are thinking. In a one-to-one setting, they are also more likely to share information with you and tell you what they think.

Delegating to the S-style

When you are delegating to the S-style, be clear on exactly what it is you are asking them to do. Show them on paper, on a board, or on a computer what you expect of them. If you do this, you can be sure they will follow through on your instructions as you would like them to. They prefer to take detailed notes so that they can refer back to them in their own time.

Demonstrate to them how far they are to go with the work that is coming their way. So if there is a cut-off point, let them know when this is. Also mention that if there is anything else that pops up that wasn't covered by you, that they note it down and go over it with you later. Mention this as it also re-enforces that you are always available when they become stuck, while ensuring you are free to do your own work without constant interruptions or questions.

Decision-making for the S-style

Although they can be quite logical if they need to be, they do listen to their feelings when making decisions, so they can be prone to changing their minds depending on what others think. Due to their compassion for others, they don't see anything wrong with making a short-term decision if it has made someone else feel better. They tend to put others' feelings first, before their own.

In a group, they listen to what others have to say and are more than willing to go with the majority. If you find this to be the case, you may need to ask them separately what they really think, away from the group. This may require patience on your part, depending on your own style. What you can do is support them in their decision making. They may prefer guidance, on a one-to-one basis, to what they can focus on when making a decision. Helping them understand why this is so and then showing them goes a long way to help them to do it themselves.

They usually require time to consider things so by going over with them beforehand what you will be covering in the meeting will give them some time to think it through. I remember a friend telling me how he needed to cut costs and was thinking about moving out of his current accommodation into something less expensive. When he mentioned as much to his landlord, his landlord quipped it was a shame he was thinking of leaving and to let her know when he formally wanted to hand in his notice. About a week or so later, the landlord came back to him and asked if there was any way she could make him stay, like reducing his rent. The landlord demonstrated an S-style trait in going away and thinking through a situation before coming back to her. A C-style landlord would have asked for all the facts before coming back with a workable solution for both. So with decisions, let them think about it and come back to you. If there is a deadline highlight this to them at that moment.

Managing their growth areas

Due to their unwillingness to challenge others, their tendency is to maintain the status quo and go along with what others are saying, even if they don't wholeheartedly agree. Maintaining relations is something the S-style looks to do on most occasions. However, growth, direction and revelations can come out of discussions that explore different avenues of thought. Sometimes, direction is needed from other sources, other than the usual figurehead. When this is so, team members can be safe in the knowledge that they have a more versatile team and if there was a need for another team member to show leadership, then they are equipped for it.

This then requires the S-style to take the initiative and make decisions. Their logical mindset is a great basis on which decisions can be based, as S-styles are generally interested in collating facts before taking action. To do this requires them to step out of their comfort-zone and into the relative unknown. With support from you, their manager, that you are willing to give them some leeway to make decisions and take the initiative, the S-style may be more open to doing so. Making the right decision may increase their confidence in taking the initiative again next time. Conversely, not getting it right might also open them up to the possibility that making decisions isn't really all that bad, especially when they have a supportive manager who is there for them.

Responding to change

S-styles are the 'change resistors'. If you look at their motivations and fears, then this is easy to understand. They like to have security and to maintain the status quo. So when there is change in their immediate environment, fear of 'what's going to happen to me' is naturally going to put them on the defensive. Communication is an important part of the change process and one way of helping them through this process is to keep communicating with them, and letting them know what you think is going on. The fact they feel they are being kept in the loop will comfort them.

Whereas the I-style is good at inspiring others in times of change, having an S-style as a champion of change is useful to keep the rest of the team calm when it would be quite easy to 'rock the boat'. And because they are good at connecting with others and maintaining good relations, having them on side can be extremely beneficial. They are the 'unseen' voice amongst the people and while being on the quiet side, they are very effective in getting a message across the grapevine.

Managing the C-style

'The devil is in the detail'
Ludwig Mies van der Rohe

Look after the pennies and the pounds take care of
themselves
English Proverb

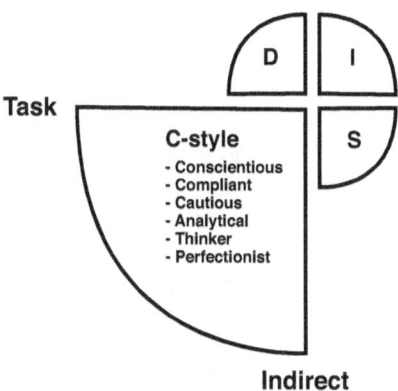

Fig. 7.4 Traits of the C-style

Accuracy and orderliness is what the C-style tends to place a high level of emphasis on. Cautious by name and by nature, this type likes to be certain before doing anything. Nothing is overlooked and every avenue of action is thought through thoroughly before deciding which one to pursue. With their penchant for wanting all the facts, they can have a tendency to delay when it comes to decision-making as they are constantly looking for more information. In fact the C-style can never have too much data. Whereas the D-style likes to cut through the detail to get to the 'bottom-line', for the C-style person, the devil certainly is in the detail.

When it comes to managing the C-style person, remember that similar to the S-style, they like to take their time and not be rushed. If you are going to delegate something to them, make sure you have done your homework and are prepared for questions. Due diligence is their thing and they have a tendency to want to take things on only if they know the state of things to the 'nth' degree. For example, the accountancy profession tends to attract many people with a C-style inclination. And when it comes to accountants, everything needs to be reconciled. If something doesn't reconcile, they will either decline to take it on or most likely request more time while they verify the numbers for themselves. The tendency is to consider everything at the outset so that they know exactly where they stand with the project they are taking on.

To manage the C-style, the two key words are: 'be prepared'. And when we say 'prepared', we mean it in the factual, logical sense. When requesting they work on something, have the facts at hand. C-styles are natural thinkers so they want to know the ins and outs of something before taking it on. Accountancy is a natural fit for this type as the kind of work that is involved would suit the way a C-style person thinks. They prefer to know everything is in its place before starting to work on it, and then improving it.

When Mark, a management accountant with a high C-style personality, took on Lucy's role, who was going on maternity leave for five months, he wanted to sit down with her as soon as possible to know all the details of the accounts she was looking after. During the handover period, he not only did this, but he also went about reconciling all the various accounts that she had. He had his own way of working and even though Lucy showed fully reconciled accounts, he still wanted to check to ensure the numbers were accurate. Being satisfied with accuracy, Mark then wanted to adjust how the accounts were organised to a way that he preferred. He did this when Lucy actually started her maternity leave. He put the data into the format of reconciliation that he was most comfortable with and maintained this format going forward.

Allow the C-style some time to 'bed in', and get comfortable with the new situation. Time is needed for them to do this as they are concerned not only about the present, but also about what happened in the past and what they think is going to happen in the future. They like to be fully prepared. However, being perfectionists, they need to keep in mind deadlines so ensure they are aware of these and check to see they are ok to meet them. If they aren't, then you may need to work with them to see where their time is being spent. Keep a focus on the bigger picture and discuss priorities, as they like to have a say in what to do, especially when they are specialists in what they do anyway. They'll be defensive toward an 'outsider' coming in and changing things, even if it is to assist them to meet their deadlines.

Be careful not to overload the C-style at the drop of a hat—they are unlikely to appreciate this. As they like to keep a laser-like focus on what they are doing, agree with them a time when you can sit down and go over certain things. If you can, send them a document that they can look at before your meeting so that they are prepared.

Additionally, being the deep thinkers that they are, don't expect them to get too excited about something straight away. They tend to approach things with caution so they like to take something away, and mull over the details.

Motivation and the C-style

Placing them in roles where they have the opportunity of working alone and where the quality of their work can be noticed will motivate the C-style to enjoy their work more, and help bring out the best in them.

An environment of order and tidiness will enable the C-style to thrive and work to their strengths. For this type, every thing has its place and that is where it should be. Slow and methodic is the way they prefer to work as they can then ensure things are done correctly and in the right way. And nothing is missed out.

Don't rush them. Allowing them to have the time to think and work shows them they have your support and confidence. If you do have to rush, due to deadlines looming, try to approach the task in a non-aggressive manner and show your reasoning for doing things in a certain way.

They like work that is clearly definable so a piece of work that can be measured for quality and accuracy will sit well with this type. They like to have the feeling that they are in control of what they are doing and can determine the outcome through their own efforts, as opposed to being at the mercy of somebody else's.

Feedback and praising the C-style

Being task-focused, the C-style likes to be appreciated for the quality of their work, and quality for the C-style means tangible results like accuracy and attention to detail.

When giving feedback, it is usually best to give it with sound supporting evidence so that they are able to understand what you appreciate about their efforts. This allows them to buy into what you are saying and for them to make up their own minds about whether they agree with what you say. Be similarly tactful when explaining what you would do in a given situation. Explain the 'why' as this gives reasoning behind your decisions. This is especially the case if the person feeding back is a 'feely' type of person like the I-style. I-styles can make decisions based on how or what they feel like doing, a 'spur-of-the-moment' thing which they just have a feeling for. The C-style person may either put up a vocal defence against your decision (out of frustration) or stay absolutely silent until they have gathered their thoughts on what to say.

When commending them, again base it specifically on what they have done and how it has helped. Be specific as they like to pinpoint where they are going right and where they aren't. They take criticism personally as they are usually hard on themselves to perform to the highest standards anyway. They relate better to accurate and specific praise since they are already thinking along these lines. So showing acknowledgement of certain details also demonstrates that you have thought through what you are saying, which they are likely to appreciate.

Everyone likes compliments, and the C-style prefers it when they are given on a one-to-one basis.

Delegating to the C-style

The C-style is a very pragmatic style so before they do something, they want to ensure it makes sense to do it in the first place. When delegating work to them, therefore, allow them to see the bigger picture. This allows them to see 'why' they are doing something and how it can be done going forward. It also enables them to make their own contribution on whether your suggestions make sense or not.

Given that the C-style has a specific way of working towards a high standard, their own standards, allow them to take ownership of their tasks. This will enable them to work to their own schedule, while meeting the goal of the overall team.

Give it to them in writing. Before speaking with them about a piece of work that you will be handing over, maybe send it to them first so that they can have a read and start making sense of it. This will enable them to get up-to-speed when you do sit down to go over it with them, and will save you time in the process. If you don't, then they will likely request this time to read and think through and discuss later again anyway.

Be clear about when a piece of work should be done by. When shown how it fits in with the overall plan of operation, they'll not want to let the team down. Being diligent about their work, they won't appreciate you too much for micro-managing them either so allow them the space to get comfortable and get on with it. See them at agreed intervals and ask them for their thoughts on anything they have found that doesn't look right.

When working on a project, this style is usually good at keeping score and making sure the loose ends are tied up.

Managing their growth areas

If the C-style doesn't feel like they have the right amount and type of information to make an informed decision, then they'll refrain from doing so. For them, decisions are based on logic and objective analysis. Encourage them to put forward a suggestion with the information that's already available. Let them know that whatever they come up with doesn't need to be final, but that this is what they think at this moment. Doing so will help them get into the practice of putting a foot forward without necessarily having to analyse the full facts. They will naturally want to look at all angles when deciding on something and won't feel comfortable if the facts presented prevent them from doing so. One way of doing this could be to help them come up with a structure for this.

Being the perfectionist that she is, Christine found it difficult making decisions without first writing down all the facts and then analysing all the possibilities. Being a visual person, and one who liked her structures, she and her manager found a model that allowed her to place decision-making into a 3-tiered structure. What this did was allow her to see that it was possible to make a decision without having all the facts to hand. It also helped to make her decision-making a kind of 'Work-in-Progress', which encouraged her to come forward with suggestions, something she hadn't found so easy to do previously.

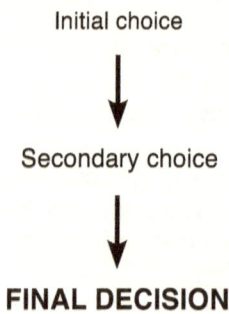

Initial choice

Secondary choice

FINAL DECISION

**Fig. 7.5 Make an initial choice first before
settling on a final decision**

Responding to change

These guys like to keep on top of things. They like to know that they are in control of whatever they are responsible for and with change, the future becomes harder to predict. As long as the

C-style is given the time to figure things out for themselves, to make sense of what is going on and to figure out strategies for adjusting to change, they are adaptable to any given situation. They naturally want to keep tabs on what is going on every step of the way. They make brilliant actuaries, accountants, analysts etc. as they want to account for everything and are good at spotting variances in the numbers, and looking for reasons why these variances have occurred.

Summary

Managing the D-style

- Prefer their own space.
- Stay firm with them and be fair. Hold your ground, be assertive.
- Don't overload them with too many details. Try giving them the big picture first.
- Set them parameters to work within.

Managing the I-style

- Put in place action points at regular intervals, to ensure follow-through is happening.
- These agreed action points should be documented and evaluated.
- Allow them the space to make use of their creative talents.
- They like to connect with others so spend some time getting to know them; it will help put them at ease with you.

Managing the S-style

- They like to be shown how to do something so spending quality time with them can pay huge dividends.
- Be patient with them, as they tend to like going through things in a step-by-step fashion.
- Be precise and clear in your instructions of how you like something to be done, then re-visit to see if they are on the right track.

Managing the C-style

- When asking them to do something, ensure you know precisely what it is you want and why.
- The C-style is likely to ask plenty of questions so be patient and ready with your answers.
- Try not to drop things on them at the last moment. If you are going to do so, forewarn them that they may be required at a moment's notice for this specific reason.
- Don't expect them to jump straight into a project unless they are familiar with it. They prefer to think things over first.

Chapter 8

Stress Management

'Without stress, there would be no life'
Hans Selye

The Collins English Dictionary describes stress as: 'mental, emotional, or physical strain or tension'.

This interpretation doesn't highlight whether it is good or bad because it can be construed as either. Stress has two sides to it, good and bad—eustress or distress. Eustress is the good side of stress, which enables one to perform at one's best and for productivity to increase. This is also known as Optimum stress (see Fig. 8.1). Distress is counter-productive and causes productivity to decrease. When stress is spoken about, it is usually in the context of distress, and therefore negative. For the purpose of this book and in the interests of keeping it simple, the mention of stress will mean distress (negative stress), unless otherwise stated.

The stress curve

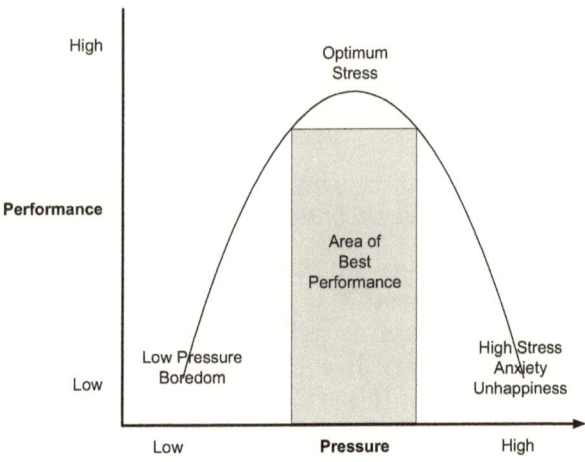

Fig. 8.1 The inverted-U relationship between pressure and performance[11]

Chronic stress (in high stressful areas) is a problem that is becoming more and more prominent in our daily lives. We cannot ignore it anymore since we are all victims of it in some way. If it doesn't impact us directly as staff, managers, directors, husbands, wives, sons or daughters, you can be sure you know someone who does suffer from it. With modern life, it has become the norm to be able to handle more 'things', whether it be juggling our activities at home and work, soaking up the constant images that are thrown at us through the media, or reacting to adhoc requests.

We only have to look at the statistics below to know our ability for a better quality of life depends on how we manage the other areas of our life.[12]

---

[11] Reproduced courtesy of Mindtools.com: http://www.mindtools.com/stress/UnderstandStress/StressPerformance.htm#

[12] All these statistics are courtesy of the Health and Safety Executive (HSE) website: (http://www.hse.gov.uk/statistics/causdis/stress/scale.htm)

'*Results from all surveys consistently indicate that stress and related conditions form the second most commonly reported group of work-related-ill-health conditions after musculoskeletal disorders...*'

'*... an estimated average of 27.5 working days lost per affected case and makes stress, depression or anxiety the largest contributor to the overall estimated annual days lost from work-related ill-health in 2008/09.*'

'*A single weekday edition of The New York Times today contains more information than an average person in the seventeenth century would have encountered in a lifetime... New statistics show that the average person in a large corporation sends and receives an astounding 177 messages a day...*'[13]

Boston College researcher Juliet Schor says technology has reduced the amount of time it takes to do any one task, but also leads to the expansion of tasks that people are expected to do:

'*In the last 30 years mankind has produced more information than in the previous 5,000.*'[14]

With the increased cost in living, many households have to bring in two sets of income as one just isn't sufficient. The list is endless and for all the things we have been blessed with in the modern age, it seems we have to work even harder to maintain any kind of sanity in our lives. The good news, however, is that we have all the tools to enable us to achieve just this—if only we knew how!

Stress is something that we haven't proactively sought to deal with, but rather something we have adjusted to in our daily dealings, as and when they happen to us. For example, at school, we aren't shown how to deal effectively with our time, to be able to prioritise, manage a budget etc. We are left to find our own way of managing to get through school and then the same again through university. As a result, we have formed our own ways of personal management. Unsurprisingly, the ways that we learn to manage

---

[13] Jennifer Tanaka, 'Drowning in Data', *Newsweek*, 4/28/98, p.85
[14] Information Overload Causes Stress (1997, March/April), *Reuters Magazine*

our financial affairs, our time and our minds, have not always been the best ways, but more often than not we have learned by trial and error through experience. Likewise, as with our finances or time, few of us have had the opportunity to receive training that can help us deal with stress effectively. And when we have the training, it's often later on in life when it is more difficult to change the habits we have already adopted. We have by then developed our own way of dealing with stress, so it's often going to take a huge effort to change it.

When detecting someone's way of dealing with pressure, allow it to manifest itself. It may well be different to the way you deal with pressure, and/or different from the way your other colleagues deal with pressure. Whatever it is, try being an observer to the behaviour. Is it work-related or something else? You will largely get the answer to this by asking the person once they are in a better place to talk about it. Being patient and understanding will enable you to better equip yourself for the different ways people deal with stress. The more responses to stress that you are aware of, the more resourceful you can be in a variety of situations.

Just as our natural way of behaving can be categorised into the DISC format, so can our way of dealing with stressful situations.

There is the D-style way of dealing with stress, just like there is an I-style way of dealing with stress. Once we are aware of the different ways stress manifests itself, we are better at doing something about it. Awareness is more than half the battle won.

Letting off some steam—The Tipping Point

We have all been to a place where the pressure has been just too much to bear—that place where one more thing will push us over the edge. Malcolm Gladwell[15] has quite aptly described this moment as the Tipping Point. When we get to this point of stress it's already too late: too late to get any sense out of the person; too late to get through to the person where they will listen to what you have to say.

When you are the person who has gone past the tipping point, the only natural thing to do is to get out of the situation. The stress has become too much to bear and we revert to our most natural style to alleviate the pressure. Regardless of our style, when we have reached that tipping point of stress, we all become unreasonable. We tend to go to the extreme of what our natural styles are:

The D-style becomes dictatorial.
The I-style lashes out at everyone around them.
The S-style will acquiesce.
The C-style withdraws totally.

None of the responses above warrant being called unreasonable as they are extreme reactions to extreme situations. They are our release responses which are ultimately there to protect us. So whatever we do, if anything becomes too much we blow off steam like a boiling kettle. However, when someone has breached the tipping point, there will always be casualties involved. Part of the

---

[15] Gladwell, M. (2001), *The Tipping Point*, (Abacus)

problem of releasing this 'steam' is that it invariably ends up being soaked up by other people, usually the S-style.

Be careful not to fill anyone else's bucket. And this applies especially to the D- and I-styles. If you can, get away from others when you feel under huge pressure and are in 'that moment'. Being a leader is showing self-awareness. When things become too much, it is easy to say something out of pure emotion which is not thought through properly, and which could severely affect the relations you have with others. So while it's tempting to want to empty our bucket, filling someone else's is not a great way of doing it. Why pass on our waste? Be mindful and patient, and take yourself away somewhere safe, away from harm's reach.

Ease yourself back in. When we are stressed and then coming down with flu or a cold is usually a good sign that our body needs rest. So give yourself this time to recuperate fully and try not to rush to get back into the swing of things too quickly. I know many people who have returned to work as soon as they felt up to it. If you took time off because you absolutely couldn't go in, you can afford to take one or two more days to ensure you are as near to full fitness as possible.

Identifying your Tipping Point

Would you like to improve on the way you currently deal with things? Try going over the following exercise.

First, visualise how you would like to see yourself dealing with pressurised situations? If you can't do this for yourself, think back to someone you know, or know of, who deals with pressure well.

Holding this thought in your mind, write this down in minute detail on a blank piece of paper, focusing on three different perspectives:

- How do you think you are coming across to the people around you?
- How are you dealing with the pressured situation at hand?
- How are you dealing with your own internal thoughts and feelings?

Once you have done this, now go over what happens when you get stressed and feel under-pressure.

So think back and on another blank piece of paper write down an occasion when you felt under pressure and how you reacted:

- With the people around you?
- With the situation at hand?
- With yourself?

When you have done this, go back to another real situation from the past and go through the same exercise. Do this again, and then again. Do you see any regular patterns occurring, or do you vary depending on the type of stress or tension you are experiencing?

Going back and analysing past situations is a good way of understanding your own style and doing something about it, if you choose to do so. Ascertaining where you want to be, as well as acknowledging where you are now enables you to check one against the other.

Here are some common reactions to stress of the various behaviour types.

Stress for the D-style:

Under extreme pressure, this style becomes more demanding—of themselves and others. The one thing the D-style wants to have is control, but when under pressure control is the one thing that they don't have, so they try even harder to get it. Due to their directness, they tend to become even more demanding than normal. Focused on action, it isn't unusual for a D-style to shout out 'do something!' to his/her colleagues or whoever is around them. For them, action should be taken! Anything is better than just sitting around doing nothing. It becomes:

'I want...'
'You do...'
'Come back to me when...'
'Let's go!'

A natural leader and 'do-er' in a crisis situation, D-styles become even more confrontational than usual to get people to achieve the target faster. Anyone who gets in the way of their target (and even stopping to question them is likely to frustrate them) is likely to get side-lined as achieving the task is the main objective. The speed of the response, and taking immediate and direct action, is the most important thing for the D-style when they are under pressure. With their increase in pace and laser-like focus, the slow-to-take-the-initiative S-style is likely to frustrate them even more.

D-styles process information fast, and even faster when faced with a stressful situation, so be prepared for a super-fast communication exchange when you see them in these circumstances. Be sure to be firm and direct, with a focus on actions and goals.

Stress for the I-style:

Being the eternal optimist, at stressful times the I-style can go further along the optimistic route and become even more positive about a situation. This extension of positivity is their coping mechanism in an uncomfortable situation. So instead of looking to deal with matters head-on, it wouldn't be unusual for them to 'turn a blind eye' to the situation and hope that it gets better somehow, especially when they don't have an answer about what to do.

When the pressure mounts, their way of dealing with people can be more severe. Being naturally expressive beings anyway, in pressured times, they have a tendency to express this frustration openly, and out loud. And the people who usually experience it, or are at the forefront of their outburst, are the ones who are closest to them. It is not unusual for them to become personal with their outbursts either. However, the I-style shows that once it is out of their system, they are able to move on quickly and they generally do.

I-styles are easy to spot when they are under severe strain as they not only find it easy to express their anguish to others around them, they also tend to spark off a lot sooner in comparison to some of the other styles.

Other I-styles, and even D-styles, will be able to identify with this style under pressure, but S- and C-styles may find it more difficult to comprehend. As a result, usually more controlled under pressure, S- and C-styles may take such outbursts by the I-style more personally. They may not be able to understand how someone could say such a thing if they didn't mean it. As a result, although the I-style will have relieved themselves of this stress, their relationships with S- and C-styles will have been affected as these two styles don't forget so easily.

If you are dealing with this style, allow them to have their release. Once it has happened and they have slept on it, it is over with and they can move on. On your part, be sure not to take whatever was said in the heat of the moment personally. This might be easier for fellow I-styles to do, and also for D-styles, as they can understand the need for this type to have their 'release'. However, S- and C-styles might find it difficult to understand how a person can just 'vent' like that, and then move on.

Stress for the S-style:

The more patient nature of this style enables them to be a stabilising influence on those around them. Calm and engaging, the S-style's natural way is to blend into the group and not draw too much attention to themselves. This is also the way they tend to deal with stress. They won't shout out like the I-style through their expressions that they are feeling the stress, or become dictatorial like the D-style. This style has an understated way of showing their stress and unless you know them very well, it's not so straightforward to detect. They'll still be their normal pleasant and courteous selves, and try even harder to come across this way when feeling the pressure inside. They will tend to do anything to help maintain the status quo in their immediate surroundings.

However, when the S-style reaches their own tipping point, there are some pointers that can indicate all is not well. Although routine is something S-styles are comfortable with, it can also be something that they turn to for solace and obtain peace of mind. So going through the motions in their work, but not actually being 'present' is an indicator.

When Steve was stressed, although he didn't show much overtly that all wasn't well, there were small things which suggested this to be the case. He'd focus on his work like he always did, but often there would be prolonged periods where he would keep his head in his work without asking too many questions. If he had questions to ask or suggestions to make, usually he would readily ask his manager or colleagues. However, this time, he seems to have retreated somewhat, and although he'd acknowledge others, he wasn't as warm and forthcoming as he normally was. Steve's work also saw a few mistakes creeping in which all added up to something not being quite right. It wasn't until his manager, Dominic, made him feel comfortable with his caring approach and patience, that Steve eventually mentioned that he was having some problems at home.

Although the passive nature of the S-style enables them to hide their true feelings well, with careful observation and sensitive handling S-styles will open up about the stresses they are experiencing. Being patient with them is the key.

Stress for the C-style:

Just like the S-style, the C-style has an indirect style of communication. They are not too comfortable with expressing themselves openly, as the I-style might like to do. However, unlike the S-style, the C-style prefers to work on their own and, taken to an extreme, can go into hibernation. Their perfectionist streak may come out even more.

Connie was going through a situation where she didn't know what she wanted to do in her career. She was disillusioned with what she was currently doing and was searching for something else. Having always come to expect high things from herself she was growing increasingly frustrated at her lack of progress in deciding what to do. So to give herself the best opportunity of making a decision, she decided to cut out all the distractions in her life and to focus solely on this one thing that mattered to her. As a result, she cut herself off from the outside world. She stayed in the comfort of her own home and even refused to see friends until a time came where she knew exactly where she was heading, and had outlined a detailed plan of how to get there

In stressful situations, the C-style person is likely to slow down even further in an attempt to understand what is going on and to pore over all the facts even more carefully with a fine-toothed comb. Their penchant for wanting to understand what is happening around them will give rise to them analysing it from every conceivable angle. So don't expect the C-style person to jump into taking action like the D-style would, or to express themselves emotionally like the I-style can do. This type would prefer to establish a baseline as to where they are now, and to understand how they got there before settling on a plan of action of what to do next.

Things to do when distressed

With so much information being thrown at us from so many different angles, our brains are wired to consume more and more. If it's not our computer at work, we are on our palmtops or phones social networking with people we know and don't know. It's getting more and more difficult to switch off as we become connected to a wider world.

To get an idea of the level of new information generated, at the Techonomy conference in 2010[16], Eric Schmidt, Google's CEO mentioned that every two days, we now create as much information as we did from the dawn of civilisation up until 2003. That is a tremendous amount of information, and as systems keep getting bigger and faster, information is going to keep coming faster, and we will need to absorb even more information. However, whilst we are awash with information from all directions,

---

[16] Techonomy conference, Lake Tahoe, CA, USA: http://techcrunch.com/2010/08/04/schmidt-data/

we still have control over our minds. Here are just some of the things you can do to keep your head above water.

Stay organised

Being organised can really help clear the mind. When the mind is under extreme stress, even the smallest of things can trigger an extreme response that, at other times, wouldn't even be noticed. Have you ever had one of those days when you've woken up and thought about that one thing that is stressing you out? You then find yourself without any milk in the kitchen so you decide to make do without breakfast as it'll take too long to make something and you really have to get to the office. So you hurry to try to leave the house to get to the office early when you discover you can't find your keys. The living room has too many of your papers spread on the sofa and floor, and the bedroom has clothes all over the place. Just this makes you wish you hadn't got out of bed and your day hasn't even begun! Not a great start.

Having an uncluttered living and working area can breathe some welcome space into your mind, especially when you have 101 other things to think about. This can make life a little easier to manage, especially when the pressure is on.

Put off making decisions

Well actually, this isn't strictly true. You do have to make one decision—decide not to make one!

Often when we make a decision under stress, we will regret doing so later. The email that was sent, the things that were said, the thing that you agreed to do but… The list can be endless. Allow the moment to pass and gain your composure before doing or deciding anything. It is usually a good thing to sleep on something, as a good night's sleep, if you can get it, can make a huge difference. With the mind clouded by the stresses placed on it, rarely can a good decision be made.

The 2010 General Election in the UK ended as a hung parliament. No outright party was the winner and immediately questions were asked about what would happen next. The usual media frenzy resulted and everyone was second-guessing what the politicians would do. Lord Steele, who was in the BBC studio with other commentators, was asked this very question—What next? He answered that they should all go and get some sleep. It was the morning after voting had closed and most likely all the leaders of the parties had stayed up throughout the night to see how they'd done. Sleep deprivation can affect our senses, so can stress. If you really have to get it out of your system, it's better to write that email, and then to sleep on it before sending. It'll most probably be modified later on, or you may decide against sending it altogether.

Sleep

Studies by Dr Timothy Roehrs, the Director of Research at the Sleep Disorders and Research Center at Henry Ford Hospital in Detroit[17], found that a lack of sleep can affect decision-making, is a major cause of accidents (1 in 4 according to the Department of Transport)[18] and can also affect learning ability. Lack of sleep or affected sleep can also weaken the immune system and lead to other illnesses.

Most studies agree that, on average, eight hours sleep a night is required, although this does depend on the person. Some people can function, without drowsiness, with as little as six hours of sleep, although most of us would be most comfortable with between 7-8 hours.

Sleep has a wonderful way of helping the body recuperate. Stress can play a big role in weakening your immune system so it's no surprise that when you are feeling the strain, you are more susceptible to catching a cold or having your system shut down in another way. Good sleep can help counteract this and enable you to feel revitalised again.

---

[17] More information can be found at: http://www.apa.org/topics/sleep/why.aspx
[18] Again, this information can also be found on the website (see note 13) under 'Consequences of lost sleep'

Reducing your intake or cut out caffeine altogether

For too many of us, caffeine has become part of our regular diet and the effects of caffeine can differ from person to person. Excess caffeine can contribute to poor quality sleep[19], affect our energy levels, interrupt our sleep and interfere with hormones in the body. We need to look at our intake of caffeine and how it affects us individually. It has been said that caffeine can stay in our system for many hours. So whilst we may feel an instant 'up' from having a cup of coffee, there is also the 'low' of fatigue when the effect of caffeine wears off.

An important factor to consider is that stress build-up is usually quite gradual, and by ignoring stress, we push our bodies further, to get us through even the toughest of times. Caffeine can further mask the stress our bodies are under, thereby enabling us to continue down a road of self-destruction until we can't ignore the signs anymore.

'Drinking four or five cups of coffee a day makes the body act as if it is under constant stress. Combined with additional work pressures, it can increase blood pressure significantly, leading to an increased risk of long-term heart disease', says a US report. Professor James Lane, who took part in the research, told a behavioural medicine conference: 'Moderate caffeine consumption makes a person react like he or she is having a very stressful day. If you combine the effects of real stress with the artificial boost in stress hormones that comes from caffeine, then you have compounded the effects considerably.'[20]

In the same article, the British Heart Foundation (BHF) says 'moderate amounts of caffeine should not cause problems for healthy people... However, some people are more sensitive to caffeine and may experience changes in heart rhythm after drinking coffee.' Eating well can aid in dealing with stress better.

---

[19] For more details on this, go to the following article: 'Managing Stress' on the University of Georgia website: http://www.uhs.uga.edu/stress/nutrition.html

[20] For more details on this article, see the BBC website on: http://news.bbc.co.uk/1/hi/health/290689.stm

Your body is more able to fight stressful situations. Try to have less tea, coffee and other drinks with caffeine, and drink plenty of water.

Ensure you get enough nourishment

In times of stress our appetite gets affected in various ways. For some of us, our appetite disappears, and others tend to over eat. By looking after your body and its nutritional requirements, you have one less thing to worry about. Stress can also reduce the absorption rate of certain nutrients, so regular exercise to go with a good nutritional diet can work wonders for the body. Exercise will also help reduce anxiety and relieve some stress.

The body likes consistency so eating at regular intervals and keeping to this schedule really will enable the body to stay energised. Just as nutrition can keep stress at bay, it can also be a source for distress. Eating at odd times (like just before going to bed) or skipping meals not only plays havoc with your metabolism, but can also affect your energy levels. Too much sugar, salt, and caffeine can also have a negative impact on the body.

A vital part of good nourishment is staying hydrated. Studies have shown that in order to stay hydrated, we need to drink 6-9 glasses of water a day (about two litres). Dehydration can be a cause for headaches and nausea, irritability and also affects our thinking. Our main cue to drink water is when we are thirsty, although studies have proven that we are actually dehydrated long before this moment.

Get into good nourishment habits as they will serve you well when you need them most. Our dietary habits can take us a long way in keeping stress at bay.

Exercise

What is there to say about exercise that we don't already know? Through exercise we reduce the risk of heart disease, cancer, high blood pressure and obesity. It can also release chemicals called endorphins into your bloodstream which give you a feeling of happiness and overall well-being. And through this, we get to strengthen our immune system which can protect us better from the effects of excess stress on the mind and body in the longer term.

The exercise we do doesn't have to be too strenuous either. Getting out and about and getting some oxygen into the lungs through walking can do wonders for our well-being. Instead of taking the lift to the third floor, walk up the stairs. Incorporating more physical movement into our daily lives can improve our general sense of well-being.

Find time to laugh and have fun

Laughter can provide both a physical and emotional release. Through laughter we can leave all our troubles behind for that moment and just live in the now. Laughter can also be contagious so when we laugh, we have a positive impact on those around us. Others suddenly feel better within themselves when they join in which enables us to feel even lighter and better. The positive impact of laughter can be explained by the chemical shift it creates in our bodies. It increases the level of health-enhancing hormones like endorphins, which make us feel relaxed and happy.

Time out

It is important to be able to switch off whenever you can. Stressful moments that come and go are not likely to cause much damage in the long run. However, where there is chronic stress, this is most likely to affect you and even cause long-term damage. The mind and body can take a certain amount of stress, but everyone has a threshold that tips them over the edge. So:

- Try to keep your home-life separate from your work-life.
- Keep your laptop, mobile phone etc. away from your bed. Your bed is not for working on.
- Meditate/pray.
- Have other interests for just you—have some 'me' time.

Summary

Learn to look out for the stress signals:

- D-styles tend to become dictatorial.
- I-styles tend to lash out verbally at those closest to them.
- The S-style will tend to acquiesce.
- The C-style will tend to withdraw totally.

Things to do when overly stressed:

- Stay organised (not easy for D-styles and I-styles).
- Sleep well.
- Reduce intake of caffeine.
- Stay nourished and hydrated.
- Exercise.
- Find time to have fun.
- Take some time out and do something entirely different.

Chapter 9

The five things that DISC is not

A method to pigeon-hole people

A label to tag against others: we are continually evolving and if we use DISC in a static way, we will find that we are not getting the best out of it. DISC is a tool, albeit a powerful one, and not the be-all-and-end-all for the judgement of others. A tool is only as useful as you make it. As mentioned earlier, just because we display one set of behaviours in a particular situation it doesn't mean that this is our one main style. A person who is a risk-taker when it comes to business can also be risk-averse when it comes to relationships. So we need to be cautious when we are drawing up our internal assessment as the context always needs to be considered.

The concept of Flow: DISC provides a structure to the process of understanding people and their styles. However, if you think this is fixed you are just setting yourself up for a fall. Nothing in life stays the same, and this includes people and their ways. However, understanding people's preferences in different situations allows us to understand them better and the more we want to learn, the better we become at connecting with others.

Fitting a square peg into a round hole

Used properly, DISC is an extremely powerful tool that can help us in many ways. However, it must also be used with caution as you could be left counting the cost in the longer term.

Ivy (an I-style) is a manager of a Marketing team at a large manufacturing organisation. One of her team members Stuart (an S-style) was on a fixed-term contract and decided that he wasn't going to extend his contract with the company, and wanted to focus on his exams full-time. He had failed his level 2 Marketing papers once and wasn't confident about how his resit would go. After discussing the situation with Ivy (who wanted Stuart to extend his contract), Stuart changed his mind and did indeed extend his contract for another six months. Ivy thought this would be the end of the situation. However, one month later, after receiving his exam results, Stuart didn't show up for work. This was out of character as communication within the team had consistently been a strong point of the group. Having not heard from him by mid-morning, Ivy tried calling his mobile, but it kept diverting to voicemail. After a few enquiries into his whereabouts, three days had passed and still no word from Stuart. At this stage Ivy was worried if he was in fact okay, and had also started looking for a temporary replacement as the work was piling up and extra resources were needed.

After a week, Stuart eventually called the office and said he had been embarrassed to call in as he had failed his exams once more. Ivy mentioned that this wasn't something to be embarrassed about, but she soon discovered the main reason for Stuart's behaviour. As he had changed his mind the first time about extending his contract, he was afraid Ivy would persuade him a second time, as she could be so persuasive in getting Stuart to do what he often didn't want.

Self-awareness about one's strength and another's weakness brings with it an element of responsibility, especially when the strength lies with the manager. Not giving a weakness of the other person due consideration can sometimes be detrimental in the long run. And what's more, it can surface at the most inconvenient moments. So no matter how influential one person can be over another, if something doesn't quite fit, it's often better not to force it.

DISC is not a measure of people's value systems

People's values are important but DISC is not a tool that looks at values. DISC operates purely at surface level which can give a good indication of future behaviour patterns, but you'll be misusing it if you want to make value judgements. There is nothing good or bad when ascertaining someone else's behaviour, it is just different. The perceptions we build are in direct relation to our own maps of the world, and acknowledging that someone else has their own way of navigating through the world can work wonders in building relationships based on mutual respect and understanding.

DISC is not to be used for manipulation

We can use it for manipulation if we like, but it doesn't serve anyone's purpose and more often than not this will result in a Win/ Lose situation. When we use it for our own ends, with disregard for others, trust is the first casualty, and once trust is lost it is often very difficult to get back. That is why it's good to share the DISC tool with your team. You get to understand each others' behavioural preferences and learn to understand each other better. Use it to foster a deeper understanding between everyone in your team. You may find team members work better with each other once they are equipped with this knowledge.

A personality profile tool

Personality is deep and entrenched. A study of personality looks at our psychological make-up and what makes us the way we are. DISC is concerned mainly with people's behaviour and behaviour patterns—the behaviours we see, and can verify. And whatever we see, put plainly, is our perception of a situation. Although we can argue that personality and behaviour are linked, we can ascertain behaviour without needing to know too much about the person. Behaviour is surface-level and verifiable. Personality is not.

NOTES

NOTES

NOTES